A HISTORY OF 24 SQUADRON

A HISTORY
OF
24 SQUADRON

BY

Captain A. E. Illingworth,

Chevalier de l'ordre de la Couronne; Croix de Guerre

AND APPENDICES COMPILED BY

Major V. A. H. Robeson, M.C.,

WITH A FOREWORD BY

Air Marshall Sir H. M. Trenchard, Bart., K.C.B., D.S.O.

Dedicated to those of No. 24 Squadron who laid down their Lives in the Service of their Country.

The Naval & Military Press Ltd

Published by
The Naval & Military Press Ltd
5 Riverside, Brambleside, Bellbrook
Industrial Estate, Uckfield, East Sussex,
TN22 1QQ England
Tel: +44 (0) 1825 749494
Fax: +44 (0) 1825 765701
www.naval-military-press.com

Copy of Message

HEADQUARTERS, 4th BRIGADE, ROYAL FLYING CORPS.

No.61. 21/7/16.

To Officer Commanding, No.24 Squadron.

....

The following message has been received from G.O.C., R.F.C. in the Field :-

"Well done No.24 Squadron in fight last night. Keep it going. We have the Hun cold."

(signed) T.M.McKenna. Captain

Staff Captain.

4th Brigade, Royal Flying Corps.

In the Field.

CONTENTS.

LIST OF ILLUSTRATIONS.

A BALLOON STRAFE.

A familiar view of the Somme country over which No. 24 Squadron worked in 1916. The escort is seen busily engaged in defending the machine detailed to attack the balloon.

BERTANGLES AERODROME, 1916: THE LAST MAN HOME.

Showing No. 24 Squadron's sheds. No's. 11, 3 and 22 Squadrons in turn occupied the aerodrome behind the railway on the right in 1916, on which No. 24 spent a few days in March, 1918. In August, 1918, No. 24 occupied temporary hangars in the immediate foreground, while No. 84 occupied the old sheds, the centre one of which was destroyed in the bomb raid.

CHIPILLY AERODROME UNDER SNOW.

At the beginning of 1917 No. 24 Squadron occupied the hangars on the left centre of the picture, with No.'s 22, 54, and Naval No. 1 as neighbours. Wing H.-Q., were in the wood and at one time the French occupied the aerodrome in the back ground.

A HALBERSTADTER SHOT DOWN IN FLAMES BY A D.H. 2.
The Somme country is seen lightly covered with snow.

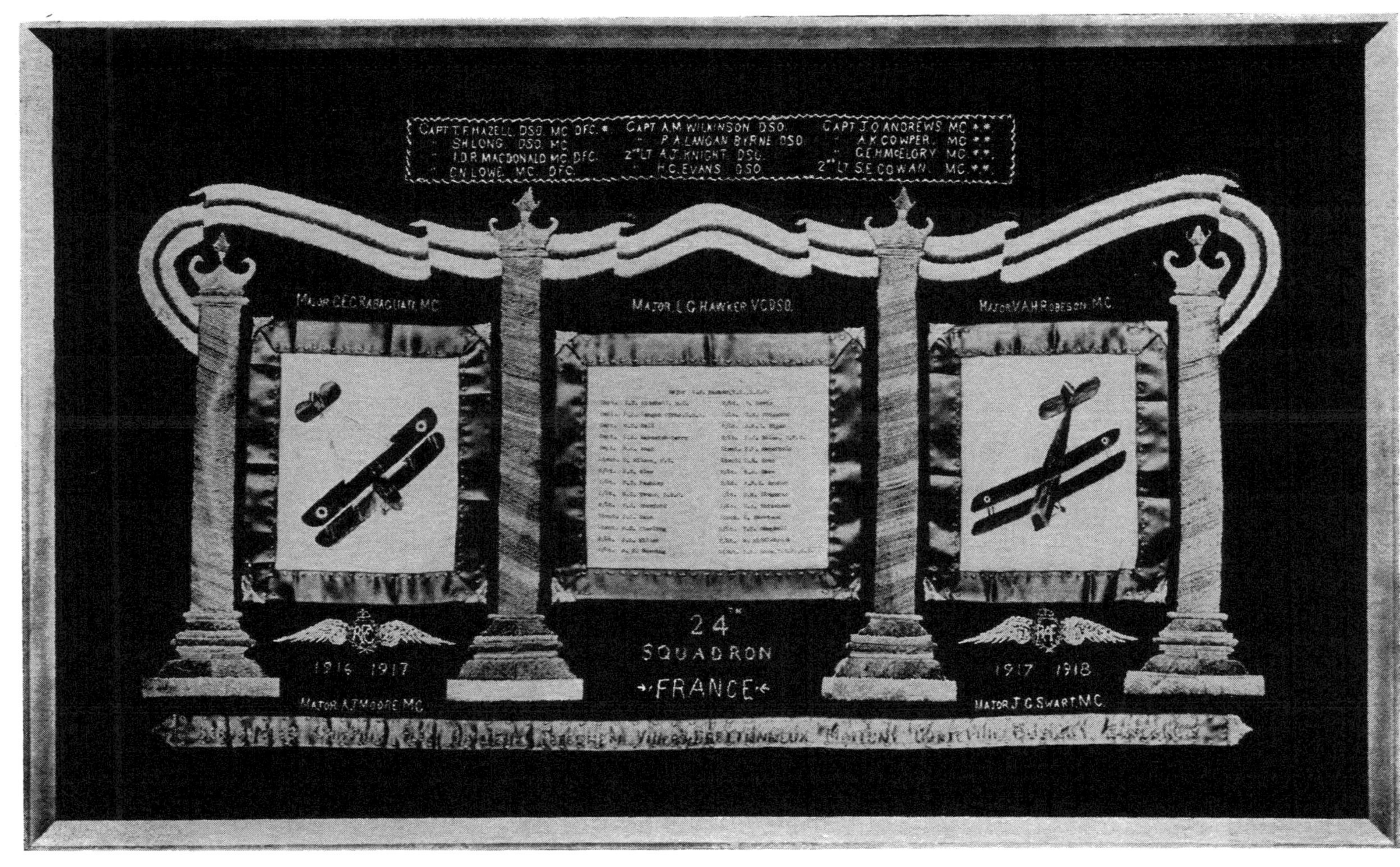

Memorial tapestry, worked by Air-Mechanic A. J. Mundy whilst on Active Service with No. 24 Squadron. It is now in the possession of No. 24 Squadron, which has been re-formed at Kenley.

D.H. 2.

Major L. G. Hawker, V.C., D.S.O., and other Members of No. 24 Squadron in 1916.

D.H. 5.

A typical S.E. 5A of No. 24 Squadron, taken at Bisseghem in January, 1919, showing the Squadron markings, flight letter and minor peculiarities such as reduced dihedral, and stream lining removed from behind the pilot's head. The single streamer on the tail denoted a flight-leader, while deputy leaders carried one on the right-hand strut. The short streamer on the left denoted an "aerobat"—a system introduced by the 22nd Wing.

OFFICERS, N.C.O.'s & MEN, No. 24 SQUADRON.

Back Row (left to right) :—A.M.'s J. S. Roxborough, W. Saville, W. D. Lusty, T. J. Moore, W. Grieve, S. R. Wright, T. Bishop, W. Thornburgh, P. E. Dennis, G. H. Fleming, W. J. Dainty W. H. Dyer, J. C. Ellis, G. Gibbins, H. Cooper, S. Gledhill, J. S. Need, Cpl. J. L. Cox, A.M.'s F. T. Ellis, F. S. Fleming, E. T. Woolfenden, C. G. P. Priest, B. L. Wood, Cpl. F. S. Cox.

Second Row :—Sgt. R. A. E. Percy, A.M.'s F. Hallam, F. Skinner, A. Hill, P. Gascoyne, D. W. Smith, Cpl. B. Jefferson, A.M.'s R. Payne, A. J. Mundy, E. Jamie, A. Crewdson, G. M. Reid, W. A. S. Allan, E. Sharpe, ————, S. Poppleton, H. Yarwood, Cpl. B. Morey, A.M.'s A. Morris, J. Parry, S. da Costa, F. W. Marshall, E. Critchley, G. Rimmer.

Third Row :—A.M.'s H. Eatock, E. L. Humphreys, S. Williamson, A. Hewitt, J. Foster, W. Wallace, G. Wilson, A. H. A. Pipe, J. Thomson, W. Atkin, W. Cannell, A. G. Herbert, P. Gladstone, W. E. Smith, S. C. Thomas, J. H. Deardon, J. Corcoran, T. A. Shaw, Cpl. V. Gradwell, A.M.'s H. C. Bowler, J. Dennis, H. Mason, Flt.-Sgt. H. Edwards, Sgts. L. C. Cox, A. Wilson, W. Green.

Fourth Row :—Sgt.-Major L. C. King, Sgts. C. H. Peters, L. Garland, J. W. Welch, H. Dearman, W. L. French, Cpl C. B. Harman, A.M.'s A. Reeves, G. W. Jones, J. R. Carruthers, E. Martin, T. Simpson, S. J. Honeywill, R. Worth, T. Spencer, A. G. Stephens, Cpls. J. Calloway, J. Cox, L. Bradbury, Flt.-Sgts. F. T. Thould, F. R. V. Tealby, J. H. Langston, Sgts. V. E. T. Hoskins, H. Brown, Tech.-Sgt.-Major F. Schofield, M.S.M.

Front Row :—Lieut. R. D. Bridgewater, 2nd-Lieut. H. A. Young, Lieut. A. A. Cresswell, 2nd-Lieuts. J. V. Flanagan, T. M. Harries, D.F.C., Lieuts. N. H. Barlow, C. A. Bissonnette, Capt. J. Palmer, Major V. A. H. Robeson, M.C., Capt. W. H. Longton, D.F.C., A.F.C., Capt. D. Carruthers, 2nd-Lieuts. A. Wren, A. L. Bloom, H. J. C. Seymour, W. B. Thomson, P. W. Johnson, Lieut. V. H. Simmers, 2nd-Lieuts. J. R. Woods, G. H. Whitehead, R. A. Eldridge, H. V. Evans, G. Abrahams.

OFFICERS OF No. 24 SQUADRON, R.A.F., NOVEMBER, 1918.

Rear row :—LIEUT. R. D. BRIDGEWATER, 2ND-LIEUTS. J. V. FLANAGAN, R. A. ELDRIDGE, H. A. YOUNG, LIEUT. V. H. SIMMERS, 2ND-LIEUT. G. H. WHITEHEAD, LIEUTS. N. H. BARLOW, A. A. CRESSWELL, 2ND-LIEUTS. W. B. THOMSON, G. ABRAHAMS, J. R. WOODS.

Front row :—2ND-LIEUT. H. J. C. SEYMOUR, LIEUT. C. A. BISSONNETTE, 2ND-LIEUT. T. M. HARRIES, D.F.C., CAPT. J. PALMER, MAJOR V. A. H. ROBESON, M.C., CAPT. W. H. LONGTON, D.F.C. A.F.C., CAPT. D. CARRUTHERS, 2ND-LIEUTS. A. WREN, A. L. BLOOM.

Lying down in front :—2ND-LIEUTS. H. V. EVANS. P. W. JOHNSON.

WARRANT OFFICERS, FLIGHT-SERGEANTS & SERGEANTS OF No. 24 SQUADRON, R.A.F.
NOVEMBER, 1918.

Rear row:—SGTS. A. DEARMAN, V. E. T. HOSKINS, L. GARLAND, L. C. COX, A. WILSON, H. BROWN, R. A. E. PERCY, W. GREEN, J. W. WELCH.

Front row:—SGT. C. H. PETERS, FLT.-SGTS. J. H. LANGSTON, F. R. V. TEALBY, SGT.-MAJOR L. C. KING, MAJOR V. A. H. ROBESON, M.C., T.-SGT.-MAJOR F. SCHOFIELD, M.S.M., FLT.-SGTS. F. T. THOULD, H. EDWARDS, SGT. W. L. FRENCH.

No. 24 SQUADRON

PRINCIPAL BATTLE HONOURS.

The Battles of the Somme, 1916.

The Advance to the Hindenburg Line, 1917.

The Retreat from St. Quentin. 1918.

The Defence of Amiens, 1918.

The Battles of the Advance from Amiens, 1918.

including

The Storming of the Hindenburg Line, and

The Crossing of the Line of the Sambre-Oise Canal.

PREFACE.

IT FELL to my lot to command No. 24 Squadron during the very strenuous year 1918, and with the signing of the Armistice it became clear that the time had arrived to collect into some permanent form the crowded history of the Squadron's career, before its members had been scattered to the four winds, and all this wealth of incident and reminiscence lost.

I was under no illusion as to the magnitude of the undertaking, but the public-spirited action of the Officers' Mess in raising the initial funds at once gave the project a real impetus, and placed it upon a practical basis which did much to ensure its final fulfilment.

I do not, however, pretend to literary talents, and I resolved from the first to act merely in the capacities of tabulator of information and trustee of the Squadron's memory.

Subsequently, through the good offices of Lieut.-Colonel L. W. B. Rees, V.C., R.A.F., I was able to ask Captain A. E. Illingworth, R.A.F., to undertake the authorship of the volume, a request to which he very generously acceded.

Although he was not directly connected with No. 24 Squadron, his previous writings gave promise that he would see the world and the War through our eyes; he had, in addition, the advantage of viewing each period in a truer perspective than could be expected of anyone who had himself served with the Squadron for a part only of its existence.

To him the Squadron, past and future, owes a deep debt of gratitude for the months of time and thought that he has expended upon the work, and the able manner in which he has accomplished a most difficult task.

Yet another benefactor appeared in Captain R. H. M. S. Saundby, M.C., R.A.F., who kindly offered us the choice of the wonderful pictures in his book, "Flying Colours," which he made whilst serving with "No. 24"; and further, he was instrumental in securing the kindly co-operation of Mr. E. G. Salmon, of the Aeroplane and General Publishing Co., Ltd., who has done much to facilitate our progress.

Sergeant J. W. Welch's contribution, "A Chronological Inquisitor," provided a means of recording the many trifling incidents which did so much to form the happy associations which all old members retain for "No. 24," and which expense would have debarred me from printing in a more lengthy form.

Brevity has, indeed, been essential throughout in order to keep the volume within reasonable financial limits. A glance at the appendices at the end of the book will show the impossibility of attempting to do justice to individual officers and men short of reproducing the entire twelve volumes of the Squadron Record Book, and much more besides.

Each may feel that he made his own special contribution to the Squadron's quota of labours and sacrifices for the Empire; whether he was a pilot facing the unlimited possibilities of the air, or a mechanic engaged in the ceaseless and comparatively uninspiring work of "keeping the machines in the air," each may look back with pride on what was achieved.

It is hoped that this book may serve to recall stirring memories to each one of those who survived, and at least be a silent tribute to those who so gallantly laid down their lives.

I must crave indulgence for any small inexactitudes or omissions from the appendices, especially in the case of events prior to my joining the Squadron. This was a most difficult part of the work, as it was only natural that the earlier records should be in a slightly less "set" form than the later ones, and that, here and there, papers should have been lost or destroyed in the oft-recurring moves.

I have arranged the roll of personnel in the highest rank each held in the Squadron and according to the date of posting to, and length of service with the Unit. Officers are arranged by flights, but, much, to my regret, the information at my disposal was insufficient to enable me similarly to arrange other ranks.

Unfortunately the list of addresses is not so complete as I could have wished. In this connection I hope that all who are not already included, or who change their place of residence, will send me their permanent addresses, in order to facilitate annual re-unions, such as that inaugurated in London on April 12th, 1919. Further, I would ask the senior members of the old Squadron in each town or district, either himself, or at least through a deputy, to organise a local annual re-union dinner. I feel that this is the only way that these occasions can be kept up effectively, and I shall be only too pleased to supply members with such addresses as I receive, for this purpose. A very little effort on the part of a few of our members would serve to preserve the bond of fellowship and would give to many others in the neighbourhood a chance of occasionally meeting old friends and drinking to "Happy days."

It has been a rare honour to serve the memory of such a Squadron, and I should like to pay a special, if brief and inadequate, tribute to the willing work of those who served in it during 1918, and to their cheerful bearing in those days of unprecedented pressure. At that time all Squadrons were feeling the shortage of men, and I do not think that we ever approached within ten of our normal establishment, whilst at the signing of the Armistice we were 26 men under strength—a deficit which was felt in every rank. For the spirit with which these little difficulties, together with the heavier burdens, were borne, much is due to the 25 N.C.O's. and men who, on November 11th, 1918, represented all that was left of the original Squadron that came out from England, and who did so much to hand down the traditions initiated by the late Major Hawker, V.C. For them and for all others who served under my command in No. 24 Squadron I have the deepest regard and gratitude for the generous and whole-hearted support I received at all times, and I wish them, one and all, the very best of success in their future walks in life.

In conclusion, I would like to tender my grateful thanks to those who contributed to this work, and to my office staff for many hours of work in connection with the tabulation of details, both before and since the Squadron broke up.

V. A. H. ROBESON.

1st July, 1920.

Royal Air Force Club,
128, Piccadilly, London, W. 1.

Foreword.

No. 24 Squadron came under my command in France about February, 1916. This Squadron was commanded by that great leader, Major Hawker, V.C., and within a very short time of its arrival in France, it showed itself worthy of its leader and maintained a great reputation through the battles of the Somme in 1916, and the still fiercer fighting of the Spring and Summer of 1917.

The loss of its Commander was a great blow, but the Squadron carried on in the way Major Hawker would have expected of it.

Its record shews what the Squadron really did.

H Trenchard

C.A.S.

10/11/19.

Author's Preface.

THE writing of a "History" is always difficult, for one has to try to be impartial without being dull. When the material from which the History has to be built up consists of a miscellaneous collection of army orders, private diaries, combat reports, and from fragmentary writings of various people associated in one way or another with the incidents to be recorded, it becomes something more than difficult.

The Author of this little work is well aware that his efforts have not achieved a high standard either as regards completeness or excellence of construction. He is not going to apologise. In answer to all criticism he must say to the members of No. 24 Squadron and their friends, for whom alone this work is intended—"You made me write for you. I didn't want to do it. I didn't want to do it."

A. E. I.

Edinburgh.
Dec., 1919.

PART I.

CHAPTER I.

BEING INTRODUCTORY.

OF all the branches of science and art which the Great War served to develop, none received so great a stimulus as aviation. From being a dangerous hobby indulged in by the few so-called reckless spirits who were willing to risk their lives or their fortunes for the sake of their faith, it grew to be one of the most potent factors of modern warfare, until—at the time the Armistice was signed—it had assumed such proportions as to be regarded as vital to the success of a belligerent. Supremacy in the air was a *sine qua non* to the success of any offensive both on land and on sea. It was the greatest of all moral factors, for while in the main the Navy and the Army of the nations engaged struck only at the Navies and Armies of their enemies (with the exception of the submarine) the Air Forces of all of the Belligerents attacked the directing centres of the nations. In all countries the civilian populations lived under the constant threat of sudden and instant destruction, and, if the fear was out of proportion to the danger, there can be no doubt that it was only a reasonable anticipation of what, had the Armistice not come when it did, would have been justified by immediate future developments.

The outbreak of the War found all countries comparatively unprepared for aerial warefare. True,—the German nation had several powerful lighter than air machines, but generally speaking they too were unprepared.

As regards Great Britain, her future Air Force was a weak and tiny infant of whom few but its parents had any hopes. Its advent had not been hailed with any unusual enthusiasm in high military circles, and its christening presents were neither many nor costly. As a matter of

B

fact, it consisted of four squadrons of miscellaneous machines, of which three were immediately attached to General Headquarters for the purposes of scouting. The aeroplanes were almost unarmed, they carried neither camera nor wireless apparatus, neither machine guns nor bombs. By G.Q.H. they were regarded as more or less useful for scouting purposes, and by the rest of the Army as rather amusing and very daring aerial pierrots.

From this small beginning there developed the mighty Royal Air Force as it was in November, 1918, with a personnel greater in number than the whole British Army at the outbreak of war.

The Squadrons were known by numbers, and had special duties assigned to them according to the machines with which they were equipped. There were bombing squadrons, reconnaissance squadrons, artillery squadrons, and scout or chaser, squadrons. In the early days squadrons had to combine many or all of these duties. Even to the end all squadrons were "fighting" squadrons. Speaking particularly, however, No. 24 Squadron was a "chaser" squadron.

CHAPTER II.

Ab Ovo.

SEPTEMBER 1st, 1915, was the birthday of No. 24 Squadron. It was formed at Hounslow on that date from the supernumeraries of No. 17 Squadron, and was temporarily commanded by Capt. Moore, M.C., but was almost immediately taken over by the late Major Lanoe Hawker, V.C. (then Captain), who was later to win such distinction for himself, the Squadron and the Empire. On formation the strength of the Squadron was—1 Officer, 4 N.C.O.'s, and 80 men, a number which, however, rapidly increased.

As was usual in those days, the Squadron was used in three capacities.

1. In settling down and learning its job.
2. In training pupils (on "Curtiss" and "Henry Farman" machines) to reinforce squadrons overseas or to complete the establishment of new squadrons about to proceed overseas.
3. In training its own instructors for night flying on "Avros," with 80-h.p. Gnome engines, and B.E2cs., with the object of using them against raiding Zeppelins.

In connection with the Defence of London, No. 24 Squadron was responsible for the maintenance and manning of the earliest night flying stations at Wimbledon, Sutton's Farm, and Hainault Farm.

Late in the year several "Vicker's Fighters" arrived, but were almost immediately replaced by "De Havilland 2" machines, fitted with 100-h.p. Monosoupape engines (at that time the fastest scouting model) with which the Squadron was scheduled to be equipped on proceeding overseas. Before it left No. 27 Squadron was formed as an off-shoot from No. 24.

The "Great Divide" was crossed on February 7th, 1916, the Squadron flying from Hounslow to St. Omer, the transport and details proceeding simultaneously by way of Southampton—Le Havre—Rouen—and Abbeville.

It was the first "Scout" Squadron to proceed as a unit to any battle front, though a few of the older squadrons—equipped with two-seater machines—had been supplied with occasional single seaters—mostly "Bristol Scouts." It was on one of these latter "lone furrow" machines that Major Hawker had already established himself as a pioneer air fighter in 1915.

The Squadron arrived in France 12 machines strong, and at a time fraught with great possibilities.

It was at the height of what was generally known as the "Fokker Scourge." Immelmann and Boelcke—the German "chaser" pilots, were at the very zenith of their power.

Flying Fokker Monoplanes, with machine guns firing dead ahead through the propeller, they had met with what in those days was considered remarkable success, and had been responsible for many names appearing in the casualty lists of the R.F.C. It was generally felt that unless the R.F.C. was to suffer severely, a very definite check would have to be given to the Germans in the air, and it is not to be wondered at that, in the Royal Flying Corps in the field, all eyes were turned to 24 Squadron under the leadership of Major Hawker, and flying the latest British machine, to see if they would be successful in administering that check.

Only two machines failed to cross the English Channel on February 7th, and the following day the Squadron was unfortunate enough to suffer its first casualty—Lt. Archer, then in charge of "C" flight, failing to pull his machine out of a "spin" and crashing into the ground. Thus was a career full of promise to the R.F.C. terminated on its threshold.

On February 10th the Squadron moved to Bertangles, taking over No. 9 Squadron's Hangars, and sharing the Aerodrome with No. 11 Squadron—and war-flying proper immediately commenced.

It is interesting to note that a certain amount of trouble was caused at first through the ease with which these machines used to "spin"—a manœuvre not at this time understood—and several casualties resulted.

Lt. Cowan did much to inspire confidence by the facility with which he handled his machine. He was the first pilot really to "stunt" this machine, and gradually the Squadron gained complete assurance.

The Squadron first drew blood on April 2nd, 1916, when Lt. Tidmarsh shot down an enemy machine near Bapaume, and from that date onward a great deal of successful fighting was done. At the beginning of June the number of machines was increased to 6 per flight, and such was the pressure of work at this time, that each flight frequently did three patrols of 1½ hours each per day.

Results, however, completely justified the effort, as the once dreaded Fokker monoplane was completely outclassed and defeated, being, indeed, literally hounded out of the sky.

Nos. 29 and 32 Squadrons commenced operating as scout squadrons further north about this time, and did much splendid work, but it was said that it was mainly owing to the efforts of No. 24 Squadron, against whom were concentrated some of the best enemy air units, that not a single enemy machine crossed the line for three whole weeks, beginning June 24th. As it was during this period that the artillery preparation for the Somme offensive was proceeding and the attack itself was launched, the importance and significance of this statement will be appreciated. Later on—in September—General Rawlinson visited the Squadron and personally expressed his thanks for its work, in no uncertain terms.

CHAPTER III.

THE BATTLE OF THE SOMME.

AS recorded in the last chapter, a strenuous and most successful effort was made by the Royal Flying Corps while the final preparations for the Somme offensive were being completed, to prevent enemy machines from crossing the lines and so divining our intentions.

It was about this time that "formation flying" with a view to collective action in attacking enemy squadrons first began to be seriously considered. One of the first tangible results of these experimental formation fights—for they had yet to be proved—took place on July 20th, 1916, when 4 D.H. 2's of No. 24 Squadron attacked a formation of eleven enemy machines, shooting down at least 3, and possibly 5, of them! The immediate result of this action was to give a great stimulus to formation flying and fighting, and offensive patrols of strong formations commenced to make long incursions over enemy territory, even penetrating to the aerodromes of the enemy, and often engaging the German machines immediately they left the ground. The morale of the German Flying Corps at this moment was at a low ebb; so much so that a change in command was made, General Von Hoeppner being appointed by General Head Quarters completely to re-organise the force.

It was during one of these offensive patrols in July that an early instance of landing in the enemy lines in daylight and afterwards flying back was recorded. Lt. Cowan, after shooting down an enemy two-seater, was diving after it to watch where it would crash, when his thumb switch jambed and his engine stopped. There was nothing for it but to land in the same field as his victim. Fortunately the bumps on landing released the switch, and he was able to take off again and fly home. Another incident which occurred about this time serves to illustrate the complete ascendancy which the Royal Flying Corps achieved over the enemy immediately before and during the Somme offensive, and is perhaps worth recording. It is entered in the record book of No. 24 Squadron by Major (then Captain) R. Hughes-Chamberlain.

"I was leading a formation detailed to escort some F.E. 2b. machines which were taking photographs, and during the course of the operation several Fokkers appeared, but kept well out of range. On the completion of the work, when turning towards our own lines, Lt. Tidmarsh, seeing a Fokker approaching a little nearer than the rest, turned on it and dived—with the result that, although he did not fire a single shot, the Hun fell out of control and crashed on the roofs of Bapaume." Fear is a dangerous enemy!

CHAPTER IV.

THE AUTUMN OF 1916.—(THE DEATH OF MAJOR HAWKER, V.C., D.S.O.)

AFTER their crushing defeat in the air during the summer of 1916, the German Air Force made a superhuman effort to re-gain its lost laurels (which had been won by Immelmann and Boelcke), to re-establish its moral and once more assert its ascendancy.

About the end of October the Fokker machine, which had been completely outclassed by the D.H. 2, was replaced by the Albatros D. III., and this proved—in turn—more than a match for the D.H. 2. In addition to being considerably faster it had a magnificent climb, and, moreover, had two machine guns, synchronised with the engine, firing dead ahead through the propeller.

In addition to supplying their pilots with this new and powerful machine, the enemy organised special chaser squadrons, piloted by officers or men showing exceptional skill, and led by skilful and daring officers. These squadrons travelled about from place to place on the various fronts, appearing wherever the pace was fastest, and were at once dubbed by our aviators as "The Circus."

One of the most famous of these formations was that led by Boelcke, who met his death in a collision during a fight with "C" flight of No. 24 Squadron on Oct. 28th. After his death it was commanded by Capt. Manfred Baron von Richthofen—probably one of the finest and certainly the most celebrated of German airmen.

It was whilst engaged in a duel with Capt. von Richthofen, that Major Hawker, V.C., D.S.O., the great leader of 24 Squadron, met his death on the twenty-third day of November, 1916.

Major Lanoe Hawker, V.C., D.S.O., was then, and had been for some time, the outstanding fighting pilot of the R.F.C.; indeed, it is not too much to say that no finer fighting pilot had ever lived. To him more than to anyone else No. 24 Squadron owed its conspicuous success, and his influence was felt long after his death. To be a member of "Hawker's Squadron" was indeed a proud boast, and No. 24 remained "Hawker's Squadron" until the Armistice was signed.

From the very first days of the Squadron's life he was its guiding star. All through the difficult period of training and mobilisation his tireless energy and inspiring influence moulded its form, and then, when the "Great Divide" had been crossed and the "Lists" entered, he was its dashing leader whose magnificent example one and all tried to follow. He had a genius for leadership and a passion for efficiency.

He was for ever thinking out new schemes for improving the organisation of the Squadron; new tactics in fighting, and new or improved instruments or weapons for the machines. How many of the devices, or "gadgets," as he called them, that later came into general use throughout the Corps, originated in his fertile brain few can tell. To mention but a few of them:—

1. The "rocking fuselage"—since universally adopted for training pilots—was first made under his supervision in 24 Squadron's workshops at Bertangles. It was used firing at targets against a railway embankment, and one day, owing to the fuselage rocking a little too much, the bullets from the machine gun, mounted in the cockpit, cut the railway telegraph wires, and the wrath of G.H.Q. descended in full blast upon the heads of the Pilgrims of Progress.

2. The "ring sight" (Major Hawker was the first to experiment in any form of ring sight which he designed and constructed himself).

3. The "aiming off" model—a device for making allowance when shooting at machines travelling at a high speed.

4. "Thigh Boots"—the fur lined thigh boots afterwards issued to all pilots, were made from designs submitted by Major Hawker.

Any number of small improvements—gun racks, engine fittings, etc., were also designed and brought into general use by Major Hawker in his quest after efficiency. In this his training as a Sapper stood him in good stead.

The story of his last fight can perhaps best be told by the other person directly concerned—the man who shot him down—Captain von Richthofen. "I was extremely proud when one fine day I was informed that the aviator whom I had brought down on the 23rd November, 1916, was the "English Immelmann." In view of the character of our fight it was clear to me that I had been tackling a flying champion. One day

I was blithely flying to give chase when I noticed three Englishmen, who also had apparently gone a-hunting. I noticed that they were interested in my direction, and as I felt much inclination to have a fight, I did not want to disappoint them. I was flying at a lower altitude, consequently I had to wait until one of my English friends tried to drop on me. After a time he came sailing along and wanted to tackle me in the rear. After firing five shots he had to stop for I had swerved in a sharp curve. The Englishman tried to catch me up in the rear while I tried to get behind him. So we circled round and round like madmen after one another at an altitude of about 10,000 feet. First we circled twenty times to the left and then thirty times to the right. Each tried to get behind and above the other. Soon I discovered that I was not meeting a beginner. He had not the slightest intention of breaking off the fight. He was travelling in a 'box' which turned beautifully. However, my 'packing case' was better at climbing than his. But I succeeded at last in getting above and behind my English waltzing partner. When we had got down to about 6,000 feet without having achieved anything particular, my opponent ought to have discovered that it was time for him to take his leave. The wind was favourable to me, for it drove us more and more towards the German position. At last we were above Bapaume, about half a mile behind the German front. The gallant fellow was full of pluck, and when we had got down to about 3,000 feet he merrily waved to me as if he would say 'Well—How do you do ?' The circles we made round one another were so narrow that their diameter was probably no more than 250 or 300 feet. I had time to take a good look at my opponent. I looked down into his carriage and could see every movement of his head. If he had not had his cap on I could have noticed what kind of face he was making. My Englishman was a good sportsman, but by and by the thing became a little too hot for him. He had to decide whether he would land on German ground or whether he would fly back to the English lines. Of course he tried the latter, after having endeavoured in vain to escape me by loopings and such tricks. At that time his first bullets were flying around me, for so far neither of us had been able to do any shooting. When we had come down to about 300 feet he tried to escape by flying in a zig-zag course, which makes it difficult for an observer on the ground to shoot. That was my most favourable moment. I followed him at an altitude of from 250 to 150 feet firing all the time. The Englishman could not help falling; but the jambing of my gun nearly robbed me of my success.

"My opponent fell shot through the head about 150 feet behind our line."

Thus did Major Lanoe Hawker die—as he had lived—"a very gallant gentleman."

During the autumn of this year a tremendous amount of work was done by all squadrons operating on the chief battle front—the Somme area—it being no unusual occurrence for No. 24 Squadron to do as many as four patrols per day. The strain thrown not only upon the pilots but the mechanics as well was very great. As regards these latter, they were often called upon to work all night, and their cheeriness under these very hard conditions was evidence of the discipline and morale of the Squadron.

The excessive work was partly due to an "epidemic" of engine trouble which developed about this time. Connecting rods snapped and cylinders blew out with alarming frequency, unfortunately often attended with serious and even fatal results.

Two splendid pilots—Lt. Glew and Capt. Wilson—were killed by cylinders blowing out and severing the tail booms of their machines, and several other pilots, notably Capt. Hughes-Chamberlain and Lt. Sibley, had the narrowest of narrow escapes.

Such incidents in a Squadron less keen than No. 24 might have gone far to undermine the morale of the pilots and to dispirit the mechanics. With "Hawker's Squadron" they had precisely the opposite effect.

CHAPTER V.

THE WINTER OF '16—'17.

THE winter of 1916-17 was a particularly severe one as regards weather. From an airman's point of view things generally were "quiet," though there were occasions when a certain "liveliness" served temporarily to relieve the "monotony of existence" as a few of the more irrepressible members of the Squadron were wont to describe it.

As a matter of fact, both sides were licking their wounds and preparing for the titanic struggle which all felt would develop before the spring offensives.

It was being generally recognised by the High Commands of all armies how vital a part aircraft was now taking in the war, and how necessary it was to achieve ascendency in the air before launching a great attack. (The full realisation of the potency of the aeroplane as a concrete weapon to be used against infantry and cavalry both in attack and defence had not yet come. That belongs to a still later period of the war.)

On December 17th the Squadron moved to Chipilly and signalled their arrival by bagging several Huns, Capt. Long and Lt. Pashley being mainly responsible for this success. On the whole though things were extremely quiet, as may be deducted from the fact that some of the mechanics were "lent" for a certain period each day to help to build what was charitably called a "road," and which in reality was to a road what a duck pond is to the Atlantic Ocean.

The long winter evenings were saved from tedium by the organisation of a squadron concert party. The following quotations taken from the diary of an officer of the Squadron typify the life and work at this period.

"Jan. 2nd, 1917.—Another 'dud' day. Very cold night; weather not altered. S. and self set off on a shooting expedition with revolvers after pigeons but are unsuccessful. It rained 'some' in the night."

"Jan. 5th.—Patrol of six scouts went out and had a hell of a fight with eight Hun machines. We drove one down, and J. was shot in the back and came down 2,000 yards within our lines about a mile from Le Forest. Long and self went out in the afternoon to get machines and find James. After being narrowly missed by shell fire from Boche we arrived. Aeroplane landed on crest of hill in full view of the Boche, who promptly began to shell it like blazes, but never managed to hit it. R.F.A. brought it back out of sight behind the ridge. We towed the aeroplane two miles back to a road. We took it down (dismantled it) and packed it on a trailer, and finally reached home at 3.30 a.m. We started at 2 p.m. Bottle of whiskey we started with we managed most successfully to smash before we drank any !"

"Jan. 7th.—Patrols of six scouts with 'L.' They all came home by mistake, leaving 'L.' by himself. No H.A. seen. 'L.' returns in a furious temper at 2 p.m., and, added to that, he got a cold lunch which made matters worse."

"Jan. 8th.—Very windy and cold day. Four machines up on patrol. All came back safely. No H.A. seen. Escorted F.E 2b's of 22 Squadron for their photographs. In the afternoon 'S.' and self went to Cachy—French aerodrome, with American Squadron—see 'Nieuport' and 'Spad,' their two latest machines. Met B., T. and J. Saw the lion 'Frisky' in the American's mess—3 months old.—Chews my finger and slobbers all over me."

"Jan. 11th.—Dud day. Very cold and misty with frequent showers of snow. The 'Wing' arrives from Bertangles and takes up its quarters 200 yards from the Squadron. No flying all day. Guns of heavy calibre firing all day long fairly pumping shells into the Hun."

"Jan. 13th.—Dud day—horribly cold. Russian Officers coming to dinner. Unfortunately I am not present, am dining with the General, with 'R.' and 'U. P.' One of the Russians has escaped from Germany twice and has a price of something over 20,000 marks on his head. He is a good pilot. *Later.* Had a good dinner with the General and came back to find the orgy in full swing."

"Jan. 14th.—Dud day. 'P.' and 'K.' go up on a test flight. Very dull day—misty and low clouds. Receive box of cigars from home. Artillery activity below normal. New battery of heavy 'hows.' stationed on our right.

" Jan. 16th.—Dud day—snow 5ins. deep.

"Jan. 17th.—Dud day—more snow. After lunch 22 Squadron invades us with snowballs. We turn out and give them hell with food and syphons of soda as well as snowballs. Put one of them in a gun pit. They depart.

"Jan. 23rd.—Twelve degrees frost. Clear day, not a cloud in the sky. One patrol under 'P.' goes up at 9 a.m. and returns at 10.50. It was supposed to escort two F.E.'s for photography, but no F.E. appeared. No H.A. seen. A.A. inactive. Second patrol goes up at 10.50 under 'W.' for escort of two corps machines for photography. One B.E. goes home with engine trouble. They escort the other B.E. and return home successful. 'S.' in this patrol has forced landing at F8d, a place S. of Fricourt. Return home in the afternoon.

"Third patrol under 'L.' goes up at 11.10 a.m. for O.P. (Offensive Patrol). 'P.' from a height of 12,000ft. sees a Hun on tail of B.E. firing at him at a height of 4,000ft. 'P.' dives with engine full on, on to tail of H.A. unobserved. Fires 15 rounds at 25 yards range. H.A. nosedives vertically and 'P.' sees pilot of H.A. fall out of his machine. He claims Hun. Not yet confirmed. This happened between Grandcourt and Thiepval.

"Fourth patrol consists of two pilots going out in the afternoon to strafe H.A. unsuccessful. An R.E. 8 crashes just in front of our aerodrome when landing. It was a brand new machine out for its first flight!"

"Jan. 24.—Fine day. 'A.' flight goes up on patrol at 9 a.m. 'W.' and 'McK.' each fly straight at H.A. from both sides. H.A. nosedives with 'wind up' and crashes near Maricourt (far behind our lines). Pilot gets out and holds up infantry with revolver. Infantry go back and get armed. Hun surrenders, but has time to burn his machine. We bring engine back to aerodrome. Several patrols went up later, but A.A. were inactive.

"Jan. 25.—Fine; 20° frost. 'A.' flight at 10.30 a.m., go up on patrol. 'Lucifer' engages another Hun with rest of patrol behind him. H.A. gets 'wind up' and spirals down, and eventually lands at Guillemont. Machine intact except for broken compass. Two-seater Albatros, brought back to aerodrome 'P.' goes up at 11.30, but has no excitements. 'L.' goes up with his patrol at 1 p.m. He engages H.A. at 150 yards and fires $\frac{3}{4}$-drum of tracer bullets into H.A. H.A. nosedives vertically and bursts into flames. Pilot and observer are seen to fall out of machine. *Later,* 'L.' engages another H.A. and fires a whole double drum. H.A. glides down and lands at Aizecourt and turns over. This makes five Huns in three days. Ten H.A. were reported as being brought down along the line this day. H.A. properly got 'wind up!'

"Jan. 28th. Sunday.—At last a few hours of rest, but I didn't go to church, as I don't quite know where they keep the church round here. The whole day was 'dud,' and so I read and smoked.

"Jan. 29th.—Two patrols go up, but they see very little activity on the part of the Huns. A.A. is extremely bad and inactive. Another fairly quiet day, but weather is foul and bitterly cold. Twenty-five degrees of frost and everyone has a red nose with the exception of myself—and mine is blue!

"Jan. 30.—Another day of sloth and unutterable idleness on the part of the Squadron. An F.E. at 7.30 a.m. flies over the hut and crashes about 10 yards from it, which put the vertical wind up us. We all rush out in pyjamas, but rush in a lot quicker to the warmth. An H.A. flies over us about 11.30 p.m. in direction of Sailly Laurette. The searchlights fail to pick up H.A. in the sky. We all go slowly, and a little sorrowfully, to bed again."

"Feb. 2nd.—Two patrols go out but visibility is poor and no H.A. seen."

It will be seen from these quotations that weather conditions were very severe and altogether against sustained activity. On the other hand there were sporadic cases of intense and acute fighting, but these must be regarded more as gladiatorial combats rather than a deliberate offensive designed to get the Hun under and keep him under. This latter object was to be attempted later. In the meantime the main endeavour was to keep up the morale of the Squadron and increase their efficiency. It was rumoured about this time that a new scout machine was to be supplied to the Squadron before the spring offensive, and flattering reports of its performance during tests in England began to circulate. Great hopes rose in the breasts of the pilots for, good at manœuvres and quick on controls as the D.H. 2 undoubtedly was, it was not a match either in speed or climb for the Albatros D III, with which practically all the enemy chaser pilots were now equipped. The bad weather continued all through February and March, and April opened miserably with two bad days.

Time was pressing on, however, and everyone knew that the hour of trial was fast approaching. It was generally felt that the spring of 1917 would witness the most determined struggle for the mastery of the air yet encountered—and every member of the Squadron felt as a boxer feels just before entering the ring for a big fight.

CHAPTER VI.

VICISSITUDES.

ON Monday, 16th April, the Squadron moved to a new aerodrome nearer the line at Flez, and on Tuesday, May 1st, the first of the new machines, D.H. 5., arrives. Here is an extract from the diary quoted in the previous chapter regarding this day's events.

"Fine day. All four patrols go out. H.A. active all day, but well east of lines. At 2.30 p.m. "C" flight dive down and fire on three motor lorries in Hunland. The centre lorry goes over into a ditch. All the lorries then stop and the men get out and jump into ditch. Also three horse transport are fired on. Horses bolt and men jump out and climb into dugouts.

"In the morning "J." goes to St. Omer for new machine D.H. 5. He arrives back at 5.30 p.m. with the machine. Great excitement."

"May 2nd.—Another D.H. 5 arrives from St. Omer. "C." and "K." both go up in new machine and land again safely."

Unfortunately the new machine was a failure, and it must be recorded that despite every effort on the part of the pilots success in any way comparable with their early efforts and results was postponed until late in the year.

On July 11th the Squadron moved to Baisieux, and the following day was an eventful one. "Five patrols during day. "A" flight on at dawn. No E.A. seen—visibility bad. "C." flight stand by 8.30 a.m. Go up after bunch of E.A. working near river Scarpe. Two E.A. two-seaters just this side of line. Lieuts. "A." and "V." fire long bursts into one E.A., which dives steeply without engine and is apparently hit. "A" flight on again at 4 p.m. No E.A. seen. Visibility fair. "B" flight on at 7.15 p.m. No E.A. seen. Visibility bad. Special patrol by "A," "B" and "C" flights at 12.30 p.m. over Albert as high as possible to guard H.M. the King and H.M. the Queen. "H.E." and "W." crashed machines on landing."

Things were very quiet on this front during the time the Squadron was operating, the liveliness being further north at Messines and Paschendale.

On September 23rd the Squadron was ordered to Teteghem. In connection with this move it should be recorded that so effective were the arrangements, the staff work, and the general organisation of the convoy, that probably no better or more expeditious move of a unit was ever effected. Over a hundred miles was covered by road in a single day, the unit moving absolutely complete.

If things had been quiet at Baisieux there was ample compensation at Teteghem. The offensive from Ypres—no longer a dangerous salient—to the sea had alarmed the enemy to such an extent that he lived in constant fear of losing his submarine bases and aerodromes on the Belgian Coast. These latter were to him of the greatest importance, as it was from these aerodromes that the machines which raided London commenced their nightly pilgrimage.

He was making a mighty effort to retain them or to make the utmost use of them before they were ultimately wrested from his grasp, and on every possible night the raiding machines set out on their murderous expeditions. He devoted, too, considerable attention to our aerodromes and dumps. On the whole, therefore, no one could complain either of want of attention or lack of excitement.

Our own machines also were doing intensive bombing, with the result that all night the drone of engines—the explosion of bombs—the boom of anti-aircraft guns, and the staccato note of machine guns filled the air.

The mechanics manned the machine guns on the aerodrome night after night without, however, achieving any great success.

On one occasion those in charge of the guns swore that they had shot an enemy machine down. It was a bitterly cold night, and the machine alleged to have been shot down was never found.

On another occasion one of the pilots observed a flight of Gothas setting out for England in the dusk and immediately gave chase, but unfortunately without any decisive result.

Early in November the Squadron experimented in carrying and dropping bombs from their scouting machines. This class of work had, of course, previously been confined to the heavier types as scouts are built for speed, and weight, as in horse-racing, is a handicap. The experiments, however, were not without results, as it was found that under certain conditions bombs carried by scouts could be used with great effect. Later in the war, notably in the last great German offensive in March, 1918, they were so used against the advancing infantry and the transport with far-reaching destructive effect.

On November 25th the Squadron moved to Marieux, and from here several bombing "stunts" were carried out.

On December 25th the Squadron received the best of all Xmas. presents—a new machine—and both pilots and mechanics heaved a sigh of thankfulness to heaven. The new machine was the S.E. 5, with 200-h.p. Hispano-Suiza engine. It was a beautiful aeroplane with a splendid performance, and was considerably better than any machine possessed by the enemy at that time with, perhaps, the exception of the Fokker triplane scout, which had recently made its appearance, and was always a dangerous opponent on account of its climb and manœuvreability. It was not, however, met with in any numbers and, indeed, preferred not to fight.

On December 30th the Squadron moved to Villers Bretonneaux.

CHAPTER VII.

"The Great German Offensive.—The Preliminaries."

ON January 26th, 1918, the Squadron moved to Matigny. By this time the pilots were getting used to the new machine, and once again they began to collect enemy scalps with gratifying frequency.

The events of the next few months are of such importance that to appreciate them properly it will be necessary to quote at considerable length from the diary of Major V. A. H. Robeson, M.C., who took over command of the Squadron at the beginning of February.

"8th Feb., 1918.—Gen. Charlton pays his first visit since I took over, and stays to tea, when the lighting set promptly 'konks,' leaving us in the dark and making a difficult situation still more alarming for me. A word as to the situation when I took over:—The Squadron had only been re-equipped with S.E. 5's during the previous six weeks and was only waiting for decent weather to make use of them. We were alone on Matigny aerodrome, eight miles S.E. of St. Quentin, and operated on the whole 5th Army front—Havrincourt to La Fére. We were in the 22nd Wing, commanded by Lt.-Col. F. V. Holt, D.S.O., who was stationed at Flez, about two miles further north, with the other squadrons (54, Camels; 48, Bristols; 8, S.E.5's), with the exception of 5 Naval (D.H. 4's), who were by themselves. The only other R.F.C. between us and the French were the Corps Wing (15th) situated just south of Ham. We were all in the 5th Brigade, under Brig.-Gen. Charlton. The German offensive was in preparation and generally expected at fairly short notice—in fact, I was at this time aware of the aerodrome—Moreuil—to which we were to retire if necessary.

"9th Feb., 1918.—Col. Holt calls and explains the probable lines and front upon which the offensive is expected, to the Squadron, and outlines our duties. At this time three schemes, called A, B and C, had been evolved to meet three possible contingencies, and these were illustrated on maps which every pilot had to know by heart. Woe betide myself or the pilot who failed to answer any question the General or the Colonel asked on the subject. These schemes were further elaborated and called W, X, Y and Z later.

"11th Feb., 1918.—Arrival of Lt. Bangs and 44 other ranks, being H.Q. flight of the 17th American Squadron. They are the first to come out and are attached to us for instruction.

"12th Feb., 1918.—Arrival of Capt. Pye Smith and the vanguard of No. 23 Squadron, commanded by Major C. E. Bryant, D.S.O., and equipped with Spads, who are to share our aerodrome.

"13th Feb., 1918.—Up to date nothing but fog and rain. A party goes to Amiens for dinner.

"16th Feb., 1918.—Capt. Ralston is wounded after getting our first Hun on S.E.'s. "A" flight go to the aerial ranges at Berck-sur-Mêr for a week's course.

"17th Feb., 1918.—Better weather and we are hard at work getting in practise on our machines. To-day I got up early to get on, but all the engines decided to fail, guns jambed and people crashed and taxied into rubbish heaps. (The said rubbish heaps, a legacy from the Huns before 1917's advance, were extraordinarily inconveniently placed at the mouths of hangars, and it took us to within a few days of the Hun re-capturing the aerodrome to remove them !)

"18th Feb., 1918.—Thanks to the better weather we were let off a four days' 'rest,' which the Colonel designed to improve our military methods on the ground, and which every Squadron had had in turn. On the whole people went to the 'war' instead with remarkable cheerfulness.

"19th Feb., 1918.—Arrival of Capt. G. E. H. McElroy, M.C., from 40 Squadron to take over 'C' flight. Having already slain 12 Huns, his arrival was an event of importance.

"23rd Feb., 1918.—'A' flight return much the wiser for their visit to the coast. The good weather has enabled them and ourselves to do lots of practise, and both officers and men are beginning to defeat the engine and other troubles which are the bogies of new machines.

"26th Feb., 1918.—A red letter day ; in the morning two flights get to grips properly with the Hun for the first time and defeat four Fokker triplanes, fighting the last right on to the ground where he crashed about four miles east of Laon, some 15 miles over the lines. Lieut. Cowper also defeated a Pfalz and shepherded it to 52 Squadron's aerodrome close to Ham, where he landed intact and put up his hands 'Kamerad' as soon as he could jump out of the machine. The pilot knew all the neighbouring aerodromes from 1916 experience and flew over several without landing because he saw the French on them and was afraid they would kill him ! Col. Holt came over about one o'clock and flew the machine to our aerodrome, very nearly meeting with an accident through the stick getting caught in the pump handle in the middle of a roll which he did at 1,000 feet after taking off—he went down on his back some way and only broke the pump just in time, while his gloves, &c., fell overboard. This Pfalz afterwards, I believe, took part in the Lord Mayor's Show and the Enemy Aircraft Exhibition at the Agricultural Hall. McElroy also made a start to-day, and later in the day we got three more triplanes, making the total for the day eight. One of our pilots, Crosbee, was taken prisoner. After dinner each of the lighting sets in the three hangars caught fire in turn, as a variation in the day's excitements.

"27th and 28th Feb., 1918.—Congratulations received from Gen. Gough, commanding 5th Army, Maj.-Gen. Salmond, commanding R.F.C. in the field, Brig.-Gen. Charlton, and Brig.-Gen. Brooke-Popham, H.Q., R.F.C.

"1st Mar., 1918.—Our first attempt to take the air in formation, 13 machines getting off in four minutes by flights. Visit from Maj.-Gen. Trenchard, accompanied by Gen. Charlton, Col. Holt and Maj. Maurice Baring. (All R.F.C. officers will realize how much Gen. Trenchard's visit at this time did to buck us all up.)

"5th Mar., 1918.—General Gough visits the Squadron. 23 and 54 dine with us.

"6th Mar., 1918.—Out of 10 Huns brought down by the Wing to-day we got eight, but had two casualties—Wigan prisoner and Clementz killed. The latter apparently shot down his opponent after being mortally wounded himself, and both crashed close together in the French lines. Spell of bad weather follows.

"8th Mar., 1918.—Four more Huns.

"9th Mar., 1918.—The whole Wing—60 machines—led by Col. Holt, attack Bertry and Busigny aerodromes during the luncheon hour. We escort 23 Squadron who, led by Maj. Bryant, attacked Bertry. The whole thing was well planned and a great success.

"11th Mar., 1918.—Lt. Cowper gets M.C.—the first award in the Squadron since we have had S.E.'s.

"12th Mar., 1918.—An Albatros D5 brought down by No. 13 Squadron is lent to us to test. Capt. Brown brings down the first Hannoveranner just in our lines. Lt. Macdougal crashed in forced landing after shooting away his propeller and getting a Hun.

"14th Mar., 1918.—Capt. Brown, Lts. Nolan (a new pilot), and Richardson, carry out a very successful voluntary attack on Mont d'Origny aerodrome, with fog at 200ft. I believe this is the first record of any bomb dropping from S.E.'s. Capt. Brown got a bullet in his boot and Lt. Nolan a graze on the neck. Joint 'binge' at the 'Godbert' in Amiens with 46 Squadron. En route I tried to find our future aerodrome at Moreuil, but though I had seen it two years previously there was now nothing left to show the position.

"16th Mar., 1918.—Exit the last of our 4-blader 200-h.p. S.E. 5's, in exchange for 180-h.p. non-geared 'Viper' S.E. 5's. We are very pleased with the new machines and are in luck in being the first Squadron to get them. Owing to our recent casualties we have only got nine war pilots left. Individual officers have earned the Army Commander's congratulations almost daily.

"17th Mar., 1918.—Gen. Charlton rings up to ask about Moreuil aerodrome which neither Bryant nor I had succeeded in finding!

"18th Mar., 1918.—Two comic crashes; 'S.' taxies solemnly into the tail of my new machine while its guns are being sighted, and 'N.' lands fair and square up our new butts, which have taken us weeks to dig—not satisfied that he was certain of reaching them he puts on his engine a little so as to ensure a good crash!

"20th Mar., 1918.—Bryant and I, with the Wing Padre 'Peter' Wilson, succeed in locating what is intended for an aerodrome at Moreuil. No hangars or tents and practically no landing ground! Lts. Nolan and

Selwyn try to repeat the raid of the 14th, but on Vivaise aerodrome. Unfortunately the weather cleared partially and they were robbed of the protection of the fog. Maj. Bryant and Capt. Pye Smith came to dinner, to which we had also been expecting Gen. Gough." But Gen. Gough could not come to dinner. Events were moving quickly. The sands were running out and the hour was about to strike.

CHAPTER VIII.

THE OFFENSIVE LAUNCHED.—THE DIARY CONTINUED.

"MAR 21st, 1918.—Woken up at 4 a.m. by 'Aircraft alarm' and a terrific bombardment, and realised that the long-expected push was about to mature. The Huns were shelling Mons-en-Chaussée aerodrome, and Nesle, some miles to our rear, with high velocity guns, making a most unpleasant noise. They also bombed Flez, but these were the nearest attempts at destroying the aerodromes, and nothing similar to the attacks at a low altitude such as we had been carrying out was tried as one had rather expected. Thick fog continued until 1 p.m., so we got our surplus gear loaded up in case of a move in a hurry. The afternoon was strenuous, as it cleared, and we got six Huns and dropped 60 bombs, sustaining another casualty however.

"22nd Mar., 1918.—Thick fog again until 1 p.m. All Squadron Commanders assembled at the Wing at 8.45 and received orders to move that day. I pushed our transport off and got some of it back for a second journey. The weather cleared at lunch-time and we did lots of flying. I despatched our bevy of new pilots with the spare machines, under Lt. Cowper, to Moreuil directly after lunch. The remainder landed there about 6 p.m. after their second job on the lines. My last remaining flight commander is wounded, leaving me with none and also no recording officer, and with a dose of 'flue' myself! The Padre has joined us and is being invaluable as a sort of combined billeting-recording-general-manager officer. Extraordinary scenes at the aerodrome—a dozen or more machines scrapping at 4,000 feet straight overhead—one fat old Hun two-seater, obviously lost, and unused to seeing anything in the air except on his own side of the lines, wandered round and round this inferno of machine-guns, and eventually toddled off west until he was leapt on by six or seven machines and sent down in flames just behind the aerodrome. Formations of Huns were much in evidence at 15,000 feet and over, but very few of them came lower, so that, as all our machines were working low, the Huns were not doing their people much good. To a large extent this discretion must be attributed to Col. Holt's air battles of the last four or five days, when No. 5 Naval were sent to bomb Busigny sidings at 11 a.m. daily, and an increasing number of scout squadrons arrived simultaneously each day to fall upon the little Huns sent up to voice the protests of the Huns underneath. As many as 100 or 120 machines were engaged in the last and biggest of these battles, and something like 16 Huns were definitely claimed, besides which there must have been many others. We were to have come in as a reinforcement on the following day, but it turned out to be the last ; the 9th Wing also co-operated in the last battle. As the afternoon went on the traffic on the main Peronne-Ham road, past the aerodrome, increased, and cavalry passed in considerable numbers. About tea time the G.O.C. 61st Division, at this time engaged round Holnon, arrived with his Staff and made his H.Q. in our Mess. The Colonel rang up about 6 p.m. to give his final orders and I left soon after with one pilot, who had come back late, and flew our machines to Moreuil, where we found the rest of the Squadron and also No. 23. We left behind at Matigny, Lt. Wilson and a rear party, who burnt all our hangars and huts, and finally evacuated about 11 p.m. At Moreuil the air was quieter, but the aerodromes looked just as animated—the Padre going round to groups of pilots just landed from the lines and all talking at once, taking down notes on the back of an envelope, from which he and I made out the evening reports. The weather kept fine, so our machines did not suffer for being in the open. Both Squadrons are billeted in the large chateau in Villers aux Arables (completely ruined later). We shared the kitchen, and the rival cooks each produced a highly respectable evening meal. Hendrie, a new pilot, arrived for us and promptly sat down to the piano, where he was kept for an hour or two while the Squadron songs were well aired. We have no telephones here, and cyclists arrive at all hours of the night with orders—we are to operate on our own, the rest of the Wing being with the Colonel at Champion, near Roye. We live, as we have been doing at Matigny since yesterday, with a cyclist up the road, who comes back every half hour to report, as it is impossible to be certain of the situation or whether the enemy are employing cavalry.

"23rd Mar., 1918.—Good weather continues, and we were ground-straffing all day, quite good targets being found on our late aerodrome. The Colonel looked in twice. The Cavalry Corps H.Q. are in Moreuil village, and we pass our reports to them. They heard of an alarm that the Hun cavalry were in Nesle—about eight miles away—at 6.30 p.m., and I sent Lt. Richardson out to investigate. He just got round before dark and dispelled the alarm. An exhausted gunner officer and seven men arrive about tea time, being the remnants of their battery—the officer collapsed soon after. A pigeon was brought to me during the afternoon by the local farmer, with a cypher message on a German message form in the case attached to its leg. I passed it on to the Army, but never had time to ask its purport. Hun machines came over after dark shooting up and bombing the main Amiens-St. Quentin road just north of us. Orders came round that the line of the Somme was to be held to-morrow at all costs.

"24th Mar., 1918.—The critical day, expecting the French to get into position. We are still losing ground, and from the air it appears as though we had either no guns or no shells—only one gun was reported, which was firing single rounds from a position two miles east of Pargny, roughly. We spent the whole day attacking the massed Huns crossing the Somme at Pargny and Bethencourt with bombs and machine guns. They had got some pretty unpleasant anti-aircraft M.G.'s there at this time too. Lt. Cowper, who has been acting flight commander throughout the last few weeks, had a very successful scrap.

"25th Mar., 1918.—Battle becoming more even, and we are not going back so fast. Arrival of French troops from the south. We carry on with the same work, keeping in the bend of the river. Cowper walks home from Cachy after the last job, as his machine was shot to ribbons. We get orders to move to Surcamps, just north of the Somme, between Abbeville and Amiens, and I despatched the transport at 7 p.m. after the day's work. However, the destination was altered to Bertangles, and I did not get the message until 1 a.m., when I sent a cyclist off to divert the transport. Exit the civilians this evening mostly carrying their worldly possessions.

"26th Mar., 1918.—We worked from Moreuil in the morning and landed at Bertangles about noon. The transport got there a little before us, after going all night—it had nearly reached Surcamps before it was diverted. We worked on all the afternoon and dropped a record number of bombs (185). Two casualties of a sentimental nature to record—old Dan, the Squadron dog, could not be found all day and had to be abandoned at Moreuil ; it is supposed that he passed away peaceably, as he was long overdue ; the second loss was a pair of home-made settees manufactured with enormous trouble in the carpenter's shop at Matigny; they had since withstood many 'rough-houses'; unfortunately they had to be abandoned in favour of more important baggage. The whole Wing is now together at Bertangles, as well as some Corps Squadrons. We slept in 'Tarrant' huts, which were apparently part of a scheme for making a semi-permanent back area aerodrome, and were fortunately sufficiently near completion to be very much appreciated. All the officers slept in one, and it is a testimony to their labours that no-one heard the Hun drop an enormous bomb, making a 12ft. diam. hole, right in the centre of the aerodrome, and only 150 yards from the hut between 9 and 10 p.m. that night!

"27th Mar., 1918.—A fuller day's work than ever—our little band of about eight surviving pilots managed to do 46 individual jobs of work and dropped 157 bombs. How the men manage to get through the work of minor repairs, loading up bombs, petrol, oil and ammunition all day and every day as well as completing each move without interrupting flying is extraordinary, especially after travelling on lorries the whole of the night before last. Things are looking up and we seem to be holding our line everywhere except at Cerisy and Chipilly, on the river. We are operating on the Amiens-Roye road chiefly.

"28th Mar., 1918.—Up to now the weather has remained almost perfect for flying and scratch camps. A remarkable fact is that up to to-day not a single machine in the Squadron has been damaged on the aerodrome since the beginning of the battle. To-day half a gale of wind is blowing making low flying unpleasant. We had one pilot wounded in the foot and another, going on his first war job, crashed and was killed, adding to an already long list of purely flying casualties incurred by this Squadron during its various stays on this aerodrome. The aerodrome has always been one of the best, and it can only be due to coincidence. Owing to the wind to-day we had a much greater amount of damage to machines from M.G. fire, Cowper in particular having the most extraordinary escapes, planes and centre section being riddled repeatedly. Rain set in about 4 p.m., and we carried out our last backward move in the wet, to a newly chosen aerodrome at Conteville, about four miles south of Auxi-le-Chateau. Except for a hurried reconnaissance by myself after lunch no-one knew anything about the place. We found what from the air appeared to be the only possible landing ground was full of huge craters which had camouflaged themselves with grass. However we all got down safely on the plough, and took up our abode at the eastern end. There were no hangars, but the Padre had secured quite a good mess-room in the adjacent farm, and had got the tents up in the orchard. The farmer was most helpful, providing a good barn full of straw, etc., for the men to sleep in. It rained like anything from then on, and I have rarely seen a more wet looking camp. (Curiously enough it matured into the pleasantest station we ever had, after a few weeks, and when, a little later, efforts were made to get us back to Bertangles on two occasions, we dug our toes in and howled until the authorities gave it up.)

"29th Mar., 1918.—Good Friday. A spell of comparative peace has set in, interrupted only by the hammering of corrugated iron and camp making in general. We kept two machines on the line all day in spite of the wind and rain, and it was quite a holiday.

"30th Mar., 1918.—Flying came to a full stop after lunch on account of the rain. Gen. Salmond and Major Sir J. Simon visited us, and brought complimentary messages from H.M. the King and the Commander-in-Chief.

"31st Mar., 1918.—Storms all day, but we got a lot of ground straffing done. The Wing H.Q., and No's. 54, 65, 48, and Naval No. 5 Squadrons are now all at Conteville."

CHAPTER IX.

AT BAY.—FURTHER NOTES FROM THE DIARY.—"THE RED AIR FIGHTER GOES WEST."

"APRIL 1st, 1918.—We co-operate in the counter-attack north of Moreuil and ground-strafe all day. Our late aerodrome there looks pretty silly already, being in the front line and full of shell holes. To-day the R.F.C. came to an end and the R.A.F. came into being ; except for the office orderly's confusion at being told to fetch the Chief Master Mechanic, upon which he produced first the Mess Corporal and then the telephone operator, the change was a prosaic affair. Redler is re-called to England, after doing marvels on a six weeks' refresher course with the Squadron.

"2nd April, 1918.—About this time General Rawlinson took over from Gen. Gough. Gen. Charlton called to-day and complimented the Squadron very highly indeed on their work.

"3rd April, 1918.—The Wing and 48 Squadron go back to Bertangles.

"4th April, 1918.—The Huns make a successful push at Villers-Bretonneux, and get through to Cachy (the nearest point to Amiens they reached during the remainder of the war). We had a very busy day ground straffing and had six of our machines shot down from the ground and crashed, but had no casualties, though some of the pilots were out overnight.

"7th April, 1918.—Lt. Nolan is missing after a very gallant scrap in which he followed his opponent right down on to the top of Moreuil Wood and then apparently hit a tree, or at any rate was forced to land in the wood. Capt. McElroy got three Huns to-day in addition to one every day on the 1st, 2nd, 3rd and 4th of the month. In several of these fights he displayed the most wonderful skill and daring in completely defeating as many as seven machines single-handed and forcing them down in their own country. One of these exploits was reported at the time by 65 Squadron. Unfortunately when coming in from the evening patrol he hit the top of a tree and crashed, demolishing a hangar and just missing my office! (He was not badly hurt, but it involved a rest in England, where he went a few days later.) Maj.-Gen. Trenchard, now C.A.S., and Major Sir John Simon visited the Squadron.

"12th April, 1918.—We carried out an attack on Rosières aerodrome.

"15th April, 1918.—Arrival of Jim, a setter, who remained with the Squadron until the end and then went on to 22 Squadron.

"16th April, 1918.—First visit from Lt.-Col. T. A. E. Cairnes, D.S.O., who is going to take over the Wing, on Col. Holt's promotion.

"17th April, 1918.—Voluntary attack carried out in low clouds on Caix and Rosières aerodromes. Exit our American flight about this time.

"20th April, 1918.—An irate battery commander sent in a complaint about a machine which performed unnecessary evolutions round his domicile, and the culprit is found to be D., so he has to go with the Colonel to-morrow and apologise. The evidence is rather amusing,—describing how the machine passed within six inches of the B.C.'s hut, and how an officer instructed his machine gunner to shoot the machine "in the petrol tank" if the operation was repeated. (History does not relate whether the gunner had any idea where the petrol tank might be.)

"21st April, 1918.—We get our first balloon, which, counted as a Hun, makes our total 100 since we started with S.E.'s in February. We have been stuck at 99 for ages. It was shot down by Capt. Johnson, a Canadian, who succeeded McElroy in C. flight. Just before we went out a big fight took place over Corbie, and Cavalry Captain Rittmeister von Richthofen was shot down and killed when at about 200 feet attacking a Sopwith Camel well in our lines. There were many claimants at the time, as the fighting was general, but I believe it was eventually decided that Capt. F. E. Brown was the victor. The Baron had about 78 victories at the time. Col. Holt and D. en route for the battery arrived at the crashed red triplane soon after, as the former testified on his return by rationing the Squadron with bits of red fabric, in spite of all orders on the subject of loot! The funeral took place a day or two later near Bertangles. I believe it is a fact that at the time he was brought down he was wearing mechanic's overalls, and except for the card in his pocket there was little to show what he was.

Col. Holt's farewell dinner with us."

"23rd April, 1918.—Col. Holt's farewell dinner at the Wing. Good show by Capt. McDonald in scrap.

"24th April, 1918.—Attack by the Huns (their last of any size on this front) at Villers Bretonneux. Our machines got off about 6 a.m. but got caught in a fog coming over from the sea and had to land at once. It did not become possible at all again until 1 p.m., and then we worked at 200ft. in the valley of the River Luce, which seems to have become our heritage for these occasions. Col. Holt gave us a final visit in the evening en route for England, after operating the Wing most of the day.

"25th April, 1918.—A very daring reconnaissance by Capt. Johnson when he flew some 12 miles over above the fog and returned under it at about 20ft.

"29th April, 1918.—We have been in suspense for several days over a threatened move back to Bertangles, while we all want to stay here after making ourselves comfortable, but the danger seems to have been averted, as we were told we could remain to-day—some other squadron evidently having stepped into the empty hangars at Bertangles!

"4th May, 1918.—Arrival of 49 Squadron with B.H.P. D.H.9's.

"5th May, 1918.—Visit from Lord Weir, the Air Minister; Maj.-Gen. Sykes, the new C.A.S.; and Maj-Gen. Salmond, our Chief out here."

The main force of the enemy had now been spent and the attack definitely held up. This battle illustrated to an extraordinary degree the vital part the aeroplane can play in the defence of a position. The advancing troops were incessantly attacked with bombs and machine guns by low-flying aeroplanes—and at night their communications continuously bombed.

At times it is not too much to say the line was held by aeroplanes alone, which, by making the roads unuseable, prevented guns and transport from being brought up.

The losses in machines and personnel were, of course, severe, but the losses inflicted on the enemy were colossal.

The material damage was stupendous, the damage to morale incalculable, but what is of even greater importance than either of these—the enemy's plan of offensive was definitely thwarted.

CHAPTER X.

"THE NEW FOKKER BIPLANE APPEARS AND IS DEALT WITH."

THE pace slackened slightly about this time and all ranks were glad of the temporary relief from working at extreme pressure. About the middle of May the new Fokker biplane began to be regularly encountered. Here is an extract from the diary dated May 20th:— "To-day we met the new Fokker biplane for the first time, unfortunately under disadvantageous conditions.

"If it had not been for a perfectly marvellous show, in which Captain Lowe and Lt. Mark rescued each other in appalling difficult circumstances, we would certainly have had heavy casualties and possibly been crippled." (Later each received an M.C. for this effort.)

On May 31st the Germans again attacked in the Soissons area, and No. 24 Squadron had to assist the French by taking over the "air" as far south as Montdidier.

On June 9th the Germans attacked for their last time between Noyon and Montdidier. No. 24 Squadron co-operated with the French Squadrons in resisting the attack.

The diary of June 17th records a typical air engagement.

"A big fight over our Villers Bretonneux between thirteen of our machines and ten Fokker biplanes, in which we bagged, amongst others, Lieut. Wüstoff. He was wounded and shot down in the French lines. Apparently he had left the late Baron von Richthofen's Squadron only three days previously to take command of another and was by way of showing how to shoot down a balloon when we blew in. This effort after the balloon accounted for the Huns' unwonted appearance on our side of the Line. Lt. Wüstoff had 27 victories to his credit, and at this time he was fourth on the enemy's list of 'aces.' We collected his machine and made an excellent walking stick out of the propellor for General Rawlinson, while the rudder and fin went to adorn our notice board. It is worth while recording that he put up a very good fight to get to his own side of the lines."

On July 26th there is an amusing entry:—"Barton and his flight frightened an old 'D.F.W.' into landing in the French lines near Montdidier—without firing a shot!! It turned out that the pilot was on his first war flight and was pretty well lost. He thought he was over Villers Bretonneux!! He had started from Peronne."

On the 5th of August there was an important conference called at the Wing. It turned out to be nothing less than the announcement of the coming offensive. The greatest secrecy was preserved, the various subordinate commanders being told the absolute minimum compatible with the successful fulfilment of their allotted duties.

The Squadrons, however, had deduced for themselves that the battle was going to be on a considerable scale, as some of the more experienced pilots had remarked on the accumulation of tanks, &c. Few, however, guessed at the real extent of the preparations or realised that the time had come for delivering the knockout blow.

CHAPTER XI.

THE LOST GROUND.

THE great attack was launched at 4.20 a.m. on the morning of August the 8th. The fighting in all arms was of the fiercest possible character, the attack being pressed with the utmost determination against a defence rendered desperate by the instructive knowledge that defeat in the battle meant definitely losing the war.

The character of the air fighting may be judged by the following extracts from a diary of No. 24 Squadron :—

"Zero hour 4.20 a.m. We put in a very heavy day in our old area in the valley of the Luce. Enemy A.A.M.G. (Anti-Aircraft Machine Gun) defence was very hot, and all Squadrons working low lost heavily. We were ten machines short at the end of the day. W. was shot down whilst attacking a machine gun battery—so B. carried on the attack, but was also shot down. He then helped W. (who was wounded) to walk back until they met a tank, which the latter got into, and B. himself found his way back to the Squadron just in time to get his leave warrant. H's. flight "bought it" heavily in the evening when they ran into forty Huns, and F.B. is missing, whilst H. had his machine riddled and every instrument shot into smithereens. No other casualties."

The Squadron reconnaissance report for the day gives further evidence of the unexampled bitterness of the struggle. "No. 131. 11.35 a.m. After engaging an anti-tank gun, Lt. L. saw some troops in "F. 14." Whilst attacking there he noticed a Sopwith Camel on the ground and went down to examine it: he was returning very low when he was hit in the main petrol tank from the ground. He landed in "E. 23," thinking it was in our hands, but he was promptly fired on with rifles. Directly afterwards 25 enemy infantry appeared 300 yards away and ran towards him. Owing to over-heating the engine was still firing spasmodically, and so picked up at once, on the gravity tank being turned on. Lt. L. shot one of the enemy with his revolver at 20 yards range, and then took off. He was just able to reach our lines. He handed his machine over to the Cavalry and gave them the location of the enemy party. He heard two hours later that they had cleared two or three hundred enemy and machine guns out of the wood."

As the attack was pressed home the enemy was forced into a rapid withdrawal of his front, which later on was to develop into a rout. The Squadrons had to keep pace with the retiring enemy, and consequently we find No. 24, in common with the others, almost continually on the move.

We will again quote the diary :—

"August 14th.—We move to Bertangles again in the afternoon."

"August 21st.—This is a very hot and dusty camp. Hazell put up a very fine show to-day after balloons, circling round the top of one while rectifying machine gun trouble, in such a way that he could not be shot at from the ground, and then shooting down another."

"August 22nd.—We are pushing north of the Somme to-day. Hazell again put up a marvellous show when sent out to keep balloons down, and deliberately shot one down under the very noses of its escort of seven Fokkers, which afterwards came down and riddled his machine with holes—petrol tank first shot—then his propellor and two longerons, in spite of which he fought his way back with his eyes full of petrol, and landed in the aerodrome within thirty minutes of starting off."

"August 24th.—Exit poor old 48 Squadron ! ! Just after dinner the Hun made a good shot with a bomb, setting their middle hangar on fire and lighting up the whole place for the remaining Huns, who burnt out all 48's hangars and melted their transport and engines down ; the stray bombs destroyed most of 23 Squadron's machines, destroyed 84's middle hangar, and made a few holes in our machines. The Wing offices were well 'ventilated' with splinters, and 23 chickens all went up in a puff of smoke and feathers.

"The Colonel and I were dining at 46 Squadron, which turned out to be about the best place to be. A concert was in progress in 48 Squadron, and the concert room was about the only place that did not get a direct hit, though the Hun shot them up with machine guns as they came out on the aerodrome. About 50 casualties all told."

"August 28th.—The Somme reached again at Bethencourt!"

"August 29th.—We are now all along the Somme between Peronne and west of Ham."

"September 2nd.—Barton and Harries made a very fine reconnaissance of the Tincourt area, locating particularly good targets for the night bombing machines."

"September 4th.—The 3rd Corps complained of a balloon overlooking the Le Transloy-Sailly-Saillisel road, so Hazell and his flight were dispatched, and within an hour had destroyed them, one falling on its own winch which burned for 20 minutes."

"September 8th.—We sent out a patrol in the morning which bagged several Huns and afterwards landed at Cappy, whither '46' and ourselves moved during the morning. (It set in to rain soon after we got there and did not stop for four days.) No hangars or mess tent were up, and there was no cover within miles, not even a tree. I have recollections of Hazell leaning up against a post with a sheet of corrugated iron leaning up against the other side to keep the rain off him. He vowed to buy a shooting stick and umbrella next time he went on leave.

"However the tent party got a small mess tent put up by the evening and we succeeded in having a regular Piccadilly dinner with fizz and filleted sole, which Sgt. Welch, who was in charge of our mess from start to finish, managed to produce. The machines had to remain out in the wet for a couple of nights. This is one of von Richthofen's old aerodromes, and the road through it is labelled 'Richthofen Strasse,' while his name is appended to various notices warning people from exploring the machine gun butts. The place is full of very fine dugouts—some 40 feet deep, and is surrounded by the old 1916 trench lines. Everywhere is littered ammunition of all kinds."

"September 13th saw two Huns shot down in flames last night. This is now a fairly frequent occurrence, as No. 151 Squadron night flying on 'Camels' have started to operate round here."

"September 16th.—Violent storm broke over the whole country and wrecked many aerodromes. Most of our R.E. 7 hangars are down and 5 machines wrecked."

"THE DAWN SHOW"— (ATHIES, OCTOBER, 1918.)

"September 23rd.—Nos. 208 and 85 Squadrons arrive to reinforce the Wing for the big push."

"September 29th.—Great attack on Hindenburg line successful. Everyone begins to feel that the war is nearly over."

"October 2nd.—We get three balloons."

"October 4th.—We get two Huns, making our total 200 this year."

"October 6th.—After some sudden changes of plan we were finally told to move to Athies—which we did to-day.

"October 8th.—Another attack for a break through. We get ground targets again like we did last March!"

"October 13th.—Germany accepts principle of U.S. 14 points."

"October 22nd.—Longton made another brilliant reconnaissance and had to report to the Army Commander in person again. A feature of our work during the advance has been tactical reconnaissance, which Captain Longton has developed to an unprecedented degree, even on days when the weather has been impossible for slower machines than the S.E. 5. Previous to this scouts have been regarded as of more immediate value for this purpose in open warfare, and many valuable reports have been obtained under these conditions; for instance, that by Captain Hazell on August 8th, when he was the first to report our cavalry in Meharicourt, and again on October 3rd his reconnaissance of Montbrehain at a crucial moment, for the Army Commander."

"October 27th.—We move to Busigny with 46 Squadron and have a common mess for the first day."

"October 29th.—Heavy air fighting all the afternoon in which we get three certain Huns and seven possibles. There were masses of machines on the line and I saw No. 1 Squadron get a Fokker in flames out of which the pilot jumped in a parachute. Night bombing unpleasantly near us."

"October 1st.—Turkish armistice."

"November 1st.—Austrian Armistice."

"November 2nd.—We are about to hand in our own armistice terms to the Huns and a big push on a fifty mile front was due to start to-morrow to help it down. It had to be postponed, however, as the French Army on our right is not quite ready."

"November 3rd.—We deeply deplore the delay as the Huns started shelling us with a small high velocity gun at 3 a.m. Most of the Squadron spent the rest of the night in the nearest trench. Performance lasted until 8 a.m., when there was a two hours' interval. A Patrol was due to leave the ground at 10.30, and after investigating the damage we got out the machines and started to fill up the shell holes in the aerodrome. However, the Huns—evidently having finished breakfast—began shelling again. The machines got off in all directions, avoiding the shell holes as best they could. So far we had only had five machines damaged, but soon things began to get warmer and the office had to be hurriedly evacuated. Just then a 15in. opened a fire and dropped five right in the middle of us without however doing any vital damage. We moved everything mobile to 46 Squadron, where we had to remain until next morning as the Hun performance continued until night fall."

"November 4th.—Battle started at dawn but weather was wet and foggy."

"November 7th.—Hun delegates cross the line at La Capelle some 20 miles S.-W. of us at 3 p.m."

"November 8th.—We have to leave the 22nd Wing and go up north to reinforce another Wing. Longton and Evans, working at 300ft. in the rain, got as far as Chimay on reconnaissance. (This proved to be our last war job.)"

"November 9th.—Our destination is Bisseghem, near Courtrai. We hear that the Kaiser and Crown Prince have abdicated and that an armistice is threatened for 11 a.m. on the 11th."

"November 10th.—Another perfectly fine day, and we are not allowed on the lines! We all flew up to Bisseghem and found ourselves in the 11th Wing—2nd Brigade. After dinner at 108 Squadron we heard that a wireless message had been picked up saying the Huns had accepted the armistice terms. Anyway, the whole country became a pandemonium of cheering and fireworks."

"November 11th.—We went up to the aerodrome only to discover that the bottom really has fallen out of the war.

"After 11 a.m. we are not to shoot at a Hun under penalty of Court Martial.

"It takes a bit of realising."

CHAPTER XII.

"Over—Over There."

AFTER the "Bottom fell out of the War" the Squadron was engaged for a few days in doing defensive patrols over Tournai and Audenarde. A few days later these discontinued, and the Squadron moved to Ennetiéres, just south of Lille. Most of the time was now taken up with sports, concert parties, and educational schemes.

On the 25th November part of the strict censorship regulations were relaxed and cameras were permitted. It was amazing how quickly they appeared. During December the pilots were engaged in ferrying Fokkers and other German machines handed over under the terms of the Armistice from Nivelles near Brussels, to Rely, near St. Omer.

During January, 1919, definite orders were received that the Squadron was to be disbanded. On the 22nd of that month the machines were flown to Izel-le-Hameau and handed over to No. 1 Squadron. As a Squadron No. 24 had ceased to exist.

On the 11th of February the Cadre left Bisseghem for Boulogne. On the 12th it arrived at London Colney, near St. Albans, and was attached to No. 41 Training Depôt Station. Early in 1920 it was reformed at Kenley.

It would not be fitting to close this brief history of 24 Squadron without some reference to those pilots who helped to make it what it was—one of the finest fighting squadrons of the war—but who did not return home.

One and all fought valiantly and cleanly for the honour of the Squadron, and the glory of the Empire, and the measure of their success is the measure of the success of the Squadron. How great was that success this history but faintly indicates, but if it should so happen that in the future the part played by the British pilots in the great victory can be apportioned, and if the achievements of the various squadrons can be computed, then high on the Roll of Honour will be found "No. 24 Squadron," and with it will be for ever associated the names of Major Lanoe Hawker, V.C., D.S.O., and the band of brothers who followed him to the "Happy Hunting Grounds."

MESSAGE RECEIVED FROM GENERAL SIR HENRY RAWLINSON, Bt., G.C.B., G.C.V.O., &c., COMMANDING THE FOURTH ARMY.

FOURTH ARMY, No. G.S. 2/10.

5TH BRIGADE, R.A.F.

The important part played by the 5th Brigade, R.A.F., in the battle of the 8th August, has filled me with admiration, and I desire to express to all ranks my sincere appreciation of the invaluable assistance they have rendered in winning so decisive a victory.

The action of low-flying machines on "Z" day, though it entailed heavy casualties, had a serious effect in lowering the enemy's moral and inflicting actual losses, as is shown by captured documents. The damage done by bombing squadrons both by day and night, the reports of the contact patrols, and the constant and hazardous work of the artillery machines had a very marked influence in bringing about the unqualified success of the operations.

I have been particularly struck by the vigour with which the balloons were rapidly pushed forward in close support of the firing line and the valuable assistance they rendered to the staff and to the artillery.

I desire to express to all ranks of the R.A.F., and especially to pilots and observers (including the balloons), my warmest thanks for the conspicuous gallantry and prowess. In no battle of the war have they taken part with greater success in dealing with ground targets, or with more credit to themselves in combats in the upper air, and I offer one and all my very hearty congratulations on their splendid performances.

H Rawlinson

Commanding Fourth Army.

H.Q., Fourth Army.
16th August, 1918.

CONGRATULATIONS RECEIVED ON THE TERMINATION OF HOSTILITIES.

His Majesty the King, to the Secretary of State for Air.

" In this supreme hour of victory I send greetings and hearty congratulations to all ranks of the Royal Air Force. Our aircraft have been ever in the forefront of the battle. Pilots and observers have consistently maintained the ever-changing fortunes of the day, and in the war zone our dead have been always beyond the enemy's lines or far out at sea.

" Our far flying Squadrons have flown over home waters and foreign seas, the Western and Italian battle line, Rhineland, the Mountains of Macedonia, Gallipoli, Palestine, the Plains of Arabia, Sinai and Darfur. The birth of the Royal Air Force, with its wonderful expansion and development, will ever remain one of the achievements of the great war. Everywhere, by God's help, officers, men and women of the Royal Air Force have splendidly maintained our just cause, and the value of their assistance to the Navy and Army and to home defence has been incalculable. For all their magnificent work, self-sacrifice and devotion to duty, I ask you on behalf of the Empire to thank them all."

George R.I.

November 11th, 1918.

MESSAGE ADDRESSED BY THE AIR COUNCIL TO THE ROYAL AIR FORCE.

Now that the final submission of Germany by the surrender of her Fleet and Submarines has taken place, the Air Council desire to express their gratitude to all ranks of the Royal Air Force for their share in the long series of operations which have ended so triumphantly for the British arms, and their deep admiration for the valour and devotion to duty which has been shown through all vicissitudes.

In every theatre of war, by sea and by land, the assistance of units of the Royal Air Force has been a factor of ever-increasing importance in the operations of the Navy and the Army ; in these islands also the Home Defence Squadrons, under conditions of great difficulty and danger, have successfully met the menace of the enemy's attack by air on the civil population.

In recent months the work of the Independent Air Force has had moral and material effects which have contributed powerfully to the disintegration of the enemy's capacity for resistance.

These results are due to the brilliant and inspiring leadership, staff work, and organization of the Force, to the self-sacrifice and daring of pilots and observers, the unceasing care under arduous conditions of the ground personnel, the courage and devotion of flying instructors at home, and to the ingenuity and industry of all ranks in the equipment branches.

To all these, as well as to all the members of the Women's Royal Air Force, the Air Council tender the expression of their warmest admiration and gratitude in a spirit of thankfulness for the great results which from small beginnings have been achieved by the Air Service, and with the hope and the confidence that, as aviation has shown itself to be so potent a factor in war, so it may also proved itself to be a beneficient influence in the peaceful development of civilization.

PART II.

A CHRONOLOGICAL INQUISITOR.

Being a brief reminder to those directly concerned in many quaint events.

BERTANGLES, 1916.

Who was the Officer who had "Old O Special" sent out from England, and what did he say when he heard that the General had "borrowed" his last bottle ?

Who shot Lt. Morgan's pet hedgehog ?

Who was the Officer who went into the Canteen in a D.H. 2, and was it for a drink ?

Where was it the Guard were always sure of an early cup of tea and why ?

Who was the Officer from B. and C. Mess who raided A. and H.Q. and got a ducking in the pond ?

Why did M. le Curé always drive to the mess on Sundays ?

And who was the officer who gave him shooting lessons with a Webley ?

Which Officer won the wager as to how many tins of "Bully" "Dan" could eat, and what was the expression used when No. 9 was reached ? And was he "Just nicely, thank you ?"

Who defeated the General and how ?

What the Officers of No. 22 thought after their attempted raid on No. 24, and how many pairs of slacks were sent to the laundry ?

Which Squadron won the "scrum" in the ante-room after the farewell dinner to Captain Wilkinson and Lt. Tidmarsh ?

Who was the senior officer who said that anybody would take him for the "Removal foreman from Maples," after seeing four lorries and two trailers loaded with officers' spare kit and furniture leave for Chipilly ?

Who's "Armstrong," got blown up by a "Primus stove" ?

What did the men think of their first real fire alarm, and what did the two officers say when they returned "early" from Amiens ?

CHIPILLY, AUTUMN, 1916.

Who was the "Surveyor" for the "Rue de Tannier"?

Who was the Orderly Officer who said "Cook, give these men 'Bully' rissoles. Can't you see that they are fed up with tinned 'Bully'!"

Who was the driver who suffered very badly from "Mag" fever?

Who was the visiting Regimental Sergeant Major who got lost on the aerodrome on account of the fog, and was found by the Guard at 5.30 a.m. next morning crawling back again on his hands and knees?—and who was the Orderly who had been detailed to show him the road?

Who won the wager the night that the Russian pilots came to dinner with the reputation of having defeated every Squadron (French and English) in France?

Why their car was still "resting" only 2½ miles away at 6 a.m. next morning?

Who fell in the ditch that night?

Which Squadron won the snowball fight?

Who was the Sergeant who was persuaded to present a new cooking stove to the Sergeants' Mess before he got "H.E."?

Who's bunk was famous for hot rum punch, and why did it become so popular with the Sergeants?

Who was the new pilot who had a rotten first night?

Who was the driver that did *not* win the motor race with the Frenchman on the Villers-Bretonneux—Amiens road?

What did the two Officers who were with him have to say in the matter?

FLEZ, SPRING, 1917.

What did the Sergeant-Major and party think of Flez when they were sent on in advance?

Where was the missing barrel of beer found when the X. Regiment had their dinner in our men's mess room?

Who was the architect of the tennis courts and who were the famous pairs at "Doubles"?

Who first sang the song "I'm a Corporal in the Salvation Army"?

Who preferred crawling into his tent on all fours, and why?

Who were the Officers who played the piano up to 4 a.m., and what were the remarks of the rest of the Squadron at breakfast next morning ?

Who was the Officer who collected "German Iron Dug-outs" ?

Who thought they were back in "Blighty" hunting when the horse jumps were put up, and what did the Dragoons think of the riding ?

Who was the Officer who secured the tiny sausage on the top of the mess tent when it was being erected, and why was it such a target for miniature rifle practice ?

Who had the nightly "firework display" brain wave ?

BAISIEUX, JULY, 1917.

Who was the "Belle" of Warloy ?

Who bought the last case of eggs for the canteen, and what did the Orderly Officer say about them ?

Who was known as "Johnnie Walker," and was it expensive ?

Who tried landing in the road under the apple trees instead of on the aerodrome ?

Who nearly shot the "smoke fire" man ?

Who "packed up" two cigarette ash trays made from shell cases from the bar when they went home on leave ?

Who "missed" the tender in Amiens and got back just in time for the dawn patrol ?

Who got all the furniture that was left behind when we moved to Teteghem, and who sold Primus stoves and lamps ?

TETEGHEM, OCTOBER, 1917.

Who put the lorry and trailer in the duck pond, and how long did it take to pull them out with ropes ?

What did the General say when he found the road blocked by the convoy ?

Who was the Officer who was pulled out of his bath and chased along the duck boards by three officers armed with two syphons apiece ?

What did the Sergeants say in the morning when they found their mess tent blown down and the beer missing ?

What did the men say when, in the middle of the concert the Major got up and said "We must stop the concert, pack up, and be away before six to-morrow morning" ?

After the Squadron had gone who were the Officers who tried to "win" a pair of crossing-gates on the way back from Dunkirk, and did the driver swear ?

MARIEUX, DECEMBER, 1917.

Who was the N.C.O. who lost a gold ring and found it two months later in his pocket ?

Who was the Sergeant who disliked "Green Strip" and why ?

Who "won" the jar of ration rum ?

Who said "Snow" ?

Who was the Sergeant who walked from Albert to Marieux up to his knees in snow rather than be late for his "H.E." ?

Who were the N.C.O. and driver who were away three days "shopping" on account of the snow, and what sort of a reception did they get from No. 6 Squadron ?

Who was the S.M. who filled the vacancy of "Bandmaster" so successfully, and which Officers were voted the best "ladies" at the concert ?

But who packed up most of the Squadron theatrical gear with that which came from London, and what was the result ?

A Squadron's thanks to the Padre who provided the cinema show.

Who were the lucky men to go to Doullens for leave after a splendid Xmas. dinner ?

Who was the Officer who was dragged through the ante-room, mess room and kitchen and thrown into the snow because he had a new "Rig-out" on, obtained specially from London for Xmas. ?

How many men did it take to catch the cock pheasant in the woods, and how was it cooked ?

VILLERS-BRETONNEUX, JANUARY, 1918.

Who sent two Squadrons to the same aerodrome by mistake, and why was our destination so suddenly changed from Flez when we had nearly got there ?

Who lost his kit bag coming from Amiens after leave ?

Who were the two Officers who always preferred to walk to the aerodrome and back from the Chateau (Bois l'Abbé), and what was the attraction ?

Who had to pay for the broken china ?

Who was the batman who was told not to laugh on parade by the S.M. and why ?

Who wanted to organise a wild boar hunt, and what did the French caretaker say about it ?

Who brought a rifle from the aerodrome for a stalk in the woods ?

What about the motor bus service to the aerodrome and back, and why was everybody in a hurry for breakfast ?

MATIGNY, 1918.

Who were the Officers who went bird's-nesting ?

Who was the new Officer who asked his batman within 15 minutes of his arrival "How many W.A.A.C.'s are there in the mess, and what sort of girls are they ?"

Who walked about the sleeping quarters during the night shooting rats with a Webley pistol ?

Whether the two N.C.O.'s had "wind-up" when the three bombs landed on the aerodrome on our fourth night ?

Who was the Officer who cindered his own hangar front ?

Who was the foreman gardener ?

What was the number of the squadron that was jealous of our settees, but failed to smash them with their combined weight ?

Who said airmen could not design and build a decent firegrate—in fact, two in one ?

Where did the hunting pictures come from ?

Who was the Officer who visited the Squadron Mess escorted by a very ferocious looking bull-dog ?

Who started the ping pong tables going ? Also the Squadron songs and the music ?

What were the ping pong tables made of, and did they stand a good test on guest nights ?

Who started two persons walking round a stick six times each, and then trying to shake hands ? With what results ?

Was the Padre pleased with his "congregation" at the cinema show, and which Squadron rescued the apparatus in the Retreat ?

Who said that the Yankees never told a lie in their letters home ?

Which two Officers sent their field boots to the Labour Corps.' H.Q. for repair the day before the Retreat, and did they ever see them again ?

What did the Canadian Officers think when the Canadian Cavalry went by the aerodrome to stem the attack ?

Expert advice wanted as to the exact amount of petrol used to burn down the hangars, and who wanted to sound the fire alarm ?

Who was the "airman" who blew up the Squadron Office with himself inside, and whether he made a good landing ?

Who were the Officers of another Squadron who took so much trouble to save their pigs ?

Was it the well-known hospitality of No. 24 Squadron that decided the Divisional Staff to "retreat" into our mess ?

MOREUIL DURING THE RETREAT, 1918.

What were the thoughts of officers and men when they saw the French peasants on the roads ?

Who said the "Chinks" were lazy fellows, but changed their minds when they saw the size of their packs on the Retreat ?

What did the other Squadron's cooks say when they found that No. 24 had arrived first and "occupied" the kitchen range and scullery ?

Who were the two Officers of that Squadron who arrived at the Château at 1.30 a.m. and were regally entertained on biscuits, butter, cheese, and a "Wee Drappie" ?

Who said the Squadron Office was well ventilated when it was out in the open with the wind blowing the papers across the aerodrome ?

Whether a piano can make cheerful music with two Squadron's pilots trying to out-sing each other ?

"Alas, our poor Dan"—*vide* Bovril Press.

Good-bye to the settees—"Firewood for the troops."

BERTANGLES DURING THE RETREAT, 1918.

Who was the Officer who asked when he landed whether he was in time for the "Aeroplane Show" ?

What did the four new pilots think of Active Service their first night in camp ?

Who was the N.C.O. who "won" the cooking range for the

Officers' Mess and the three cooking stoves for the men before leaving for Conteville, and whether anyone ever found out ?

What Squadron left the crashed S.E. 5 on the aerodrome, and was it because it used to belong to 24 that they had put a notice inside to say it was not safe to "stunt" it ?

Whether anybody was not tired at this time, and if not, why not ?

CONTEVILLE, 1918.

Who was the N.C.O. who was responsible for erecting the officers' sleeping tents in such perfectly straight lines ?

Who told the General that he was improperly dressed, and also gave a famous lecture on synchronised Lewis guns ?

Who invited the lady visitors to the ante-room ?

Who were the stranded motorists from another Squadron who had to be "bedded" in the straw barn for lack of accommodation ?

Who won the most games of "Bumple-puppy" ?

Why did the Canadians prefer "Rounders" to "Baseball," and was it because the ball was softer ?

What about the International Matches ?

Who was the Officer who gave three days' hard digging as a certain cure for a "livver" ?

Who threatened to shoot the magpie if it came into his tent again early in the morning and woke him up (especially when not on early flying) ?

Who was the genial Officer who was invited to mess with No. 24, and what polish did he use on his Sam Brown and gaiters ?

Who said the Squadron could not have a real good dinner and a concert out of the canteen funds ?

Why did Air-Mechanic Yarwood dress up his doll like a pilot, and why did his hat always fall off ?

Who taught him the expression "I'll slosh it across yer," and why did he always cry when singing "Oh Lucky Jim" ?

Who enticed "Jim" away from the Lorry Park, and what did "Jock Wock," say about him when he arrived from No. 46 Squadron ?

Who was the mechanic who dressed "Titch" up in football clothes and said he was to be the captain of the team, and what did the N.C.O. say ?

How many officers and men did *not* avail themselves of a flight in a "Jerry" 2-seater ?

Who was the driver who had a passion for dogs, and where did he get the one he was so fond of taking out in the touring car ?

Why was it called "Chips" ?—after "Wood," I suppose.

Who had a brain-wave—"Kit inspection ! "—the second during the life of the Squadron in France ?

The Men's Library voted a success.

BERTANGLES, AUGUST, 1918.

What a rotten camp after Conteville !

Who said the mess-room would make a good dancing tent if, after a game of cricket, the "stumps" were pulled up ?

Who said what when the model of a "Camel" was "pinched" for a joke ?

Who says there is no excitement at a concert when "Jerry" is handy dropping bombs ?

Who were the two Officers found lying in a trench wearing tin hats ?

How far did the electrician walk that night ?

Who wanted to start a small museum of German machine guns, bombs, bayonettes, &c., and why were some always to be found on the ante-room floor ?

What did H.Q. workshops say when the Camel arrived ?

Has anybody here seen "Amy" ?

CAPPY, SEPTEMBER, 1918.

Who said airmen never lived in dug-outs ?

What did the clerks say when the office blew down in a storm one night ?

Which Officer was having a bath when the tent blew over ?

Whether the Officers found bomb throwing as good fun as the men found rifle shooting, with "Jerry" ammunition ?

Who found out where to buy "Veuve Cliquot" bubbly at 18 francs a bottle ? Was it "good value" ?

Who said "Beer and sausages" when the "fat little Hun" came down doing "old man turns" ? "And rightly so !'"

ATHIES, OCTOBER, 1918.

Who was the inventor of squibs ? "

The name is wanted of the composer of the famous Band March, "For we belong to twenty-four" ?

Did our neighbours object to our nocturnal Band Parades, and was that why they kicked one side out of the ante-room ?

Who was the Officer who had to make his speech from the ping-pong table the night before he left to take command of a Squadron of his own, and whether the electric light wires were useful ?

Who felt "incredibly old and incredibly decrepit"—in fact, "Hundreds of years old" ?

Which Squadron's dog won the first round ?—"Jim" seemed happy ?

Who was the Officer from another Squadron who tried to "win" the mess's tame lark ?

Men's smoking concert voted a huge success. Everybody sober and just, but who fell into the petrol dump and was fished out by the man in charge next morning ?

BUSIGNY, NOVEMBER, 1918.

What did the S.M. say when he failed to find the new aerodrome and meet his C.O. there ?

Why was "Jock Wock's" kennel put beside the entrance to the ante-room, and was it to keep tramps away ?

What was it at the back of the camp that was described as "a bit mellow" ?—excepting "Jock Wock," of course !

Who were the Officers who, when invited out to dinner, took with them a hot roast joint and a "Dicksee" of potatotes ?

What made "Jerry" so spiteful that he threw shells at the aerodrome ? Was it "S.E. 5 fever," and had the "little old man" seen us coming" ?

Definition of "Brothers in Arms"—two squadrons living and sleeping in enough space for one.

Who reported a Hun as "all hair and teeth, with eyes sticking out on straws" ?—and was it "the material to administer" ?

BISSEGHEM, NOVEMBER, 1918.

First night there "Armistice" night.

Who swore bcause it was such a "dry" night—nothing unpacked ?

Who dug out the band, and where were the instruments found next day ?

Did anybody see a fireworks display ?

Who said "Very lights" ?

Did any china get broken when the mess lorry fell into the canal, and what did the passengers think about it ?

ENNETIERES, NOVEMBER, 1918.

Who said the change from War to Peace made no difference ? Look at the footer matches, Rugby, pleasure trips, not to mention ping-pong tournaments, with "physical jerks" and drill thrown in ?

Who said Squadron Photographs ?

Who was the Officer of another Corps who wrote in the Mess Suggestion Book the following advice to his own officers when visiting No. 24 Squadron:—"Try and remember that flying starts very early in the mornings, and that staying up with your hosts until early morning is bad for pilots' nerves !" ?

Who said "What ho for Brussels" ! and was anybody keen to go ?

How many men got into Lille without permits ?

Who christened the famous football teams, "Bradbury's Lay 'em outs" and "Jefferson's Stiffen 'ems" ? and which team won ?

Hard lines not winning the cup, 24 !

BISSEGHEM, DECEMBER, 1918.

Who was Martha, and who was the attraction ?

Who was stage carpenter and scene painter ?

"Sports voted a huge success," thanks to the Committee ?

Who first invited ladies to the concerts ?

Who were the first lucky men to be demobilized ?

Who drove the tender to Courtrai and back on Christmas Day ?

What about the "Wandering Minstrels" ?

"Pilots wanted for the Rhine and for Russia"—who went to Russia ?

Who was it that should have been a second-hand dealer ?

Who was the auctioneer and clerk to the Officers' mess sale ?

Why did the gramaphone make a "Record" ?

Who said "Models"—not ladies but aeroplanes ?

What hopes did the Cadre have when the rest of the Squadron was disbanded and sent to "Le Petit Ronchin," leaving them high and dry ?

Who put a cross on the burning rubbish heap the day before the Squadron left, with these words chalked on it :—"Here lies the Remains of Good Old Twenty-four ; born October, 1915, died February, 1919" ?

Lastly, was everyone satisfied ? The war was over, flying finished.—No more early calls, no more "joy-rides," no more crashes, no more drinks or cocoas hot ; the concerts stopped, the stage down, the canteen closed, the sports kit sold, the piano gone, and the library, till only the poor old black cat is left behind. Let's hope some-one to him will be kind, and so

"Some lucky lads will to "Blighty" go,
Others on the Rhine their face must show,
But high or low, where ever they go,
Twenty-four will be their one great show."

J. W. W.

Per Ardua ad Astra.

PART III.

Pro Patria Mori.

ROLL OF HONOUR.

KILLED IN ACTION.

2nd-Lt. K. P. McNamara	20 June, 1916.
Lt. D. H. Gray	3 July, ,,
2nd-Lt. H. C. Evans, D.S.O.	8 Sept., ,,
Lt. N. P. Manfield	9 Sept., ,,
Lt. P. Langan Bryne, D.S.O.	16 Oct., ,,
2nd-Lt. W. C. Crawford	17 Nov., ,,
2nd-Lt. H. B. Begg	23 Nov., ,,
Maj. L. G. Hawker, V.C., D.S.O.	23 Nov., ,,
2nd-Lt. E. Lewis	26 Dec., ,,
2nd-Lt. J. K. Ross	5 April, 1917.
2nd-Lt. M. A. White	23 April, ,,
Lt. H. C. Cutler	10 May, ,,
Capt. H. E. Read	10 Aug., 1917.
2nd-Lt. J. G. White	26 Sept., ,,
2nd-Lt. G. W. Forbes	18 Oct., ,,
2nd-Lt. I. D. Campbell	30 Nov., ,,
Lt. D. N. Ross, D.C.M., M.M.	17 Feb., 1918.
2nd-Lt. W. F. Poulter	5 Mar., ,,
2nd-Lt. D. M. Clementz	6 Mar., ,,
2nd-Lt. E. A. Whitehead	13 Mar., ,,
2nd-Lt. P. J. Nolan, D.F.C.	7 April, ,,
2nd-Lt. E. Harrison	17 May, ,,
2nd-Lt. J. J. Dawe	7 June, ,,
Lt. W. C. Sterling	3 Oct., ,,

ACCIDENTALLY KILLED WHILST FLYING.

2nd-Lt. A. E. C. Archer	9 Feb., 1916.
2nd-Lt. E. A. Cave	13 Feb., ,,
Capt. E. H. Mitchell, M.C.	22 April, ,,
2nd-Lt. G. Wigglesworth	8 July, ,,
Lt. D. Wilson, M.C.	30 July, ,,
2nd-Lt. A. E. Glew	8 Sept., ,,
2nd-Lt. E. C. Pashley	17 Mar., 1917.
2nd-Lt. E. Kent	8 April, ,,
Capt. W. T. Hall	19 June, ,,
Capt. L. A. Hardwick-Terry	31 Aug., 1917.
Lt. A. W. Peacock	9 Sept., ,,
2nd-Lt. N. H. Albury	15 Sept., ,,
2nd-Lt. R. G. M. McRae	28 Jan., 1918.
2nd-Lt. J. A. Miller	28 Mar., ,,
Lt. J. A. E. R. Daley, D.F.C. (died of injuries)	8 July, ,,
2nd-Lt. J. S. Haigh	15 Aug., ,,
Lt. R. A. Pertus	29 Aug., ,,

MISSING (Fate Unknown).

2nd-Lt. R. H. Kirkaldy	26 Mar., 1918.
2nd-Lt. W. J. Miller	17 Sept., ,,
2nd-Lt. E. Carpenter	3 Oct., 1918.

WOUNDED.

Capt. R. E. A. W. Hughes-Chamberlain	16 Aug., 1916.
2nd-Lt. S. J. Sibley	26 Aug., ,,
2nd-Lt. C. P. V. Roche	30 Sept., ,,
1941 Sgt. Cockerell, S.	10 Oct., ,,
Lt. W. F. T. James	5 Jan., 1917.
Capt. H. W. C. Jones	21 Mar., ,,
Capt. L. V. Thorowgood	21 Sept., ,,
2nd-Lt. R. C. Davies	2 Oct., ,,
2nd-Lt. W. J. Statham	8 Nov., ,,
Capt. J. S. Ralston, M.C.	16 Feb., 1918.
2nd-Lt. P. A. MacDougall, M.C.	12 Mar., ,,
2nd-Lt. P. J. Nolan, D.F.C.	14 Mar., ,,
Lt. H. V. L. Tubbs	21 Mar., ,,
Capt. B. P. G. Beanlands, M.C.	22 Mar., ,,
2nd-Lt. W. F. Warner	24 Mar., ,,
Lt. F. B. Heakes	28 Mar., ,,
2nd-Lt. E. T. Hendrie	12 April, ,,
Lt. E. B. Wilson	25 June, ,,
2nd-Lt. J. R. Watkins	8 Aug., ,,

PRISONERS OF WAR.

Name	Date
2nd-Lt. O. Lerwill	26 Mar., 1916.
2nd-Lt. C. Kerr	11 July, ,,
Lt. L. R. Briggs	11 Sept., ,,
2nd-Lt. J. V. Bowring	14 Sept., ,,
2nd-Lt. N. Middlebrook	10 Oct., ,,
Lt. J. H. Goodall	24 April, 1917.
2nd-Lt. G. P. Robertson	10 Sept., ,,
2nd-Lt. A. Taylor	26 Sept., 1917.
2nd-Lt. C. H. Crosbee (wounded)	26 Feb., 1918.
2nd-Lt. A. P. C. Wigan	8 Mar., ,,
Lt. R. A. Slipper (wounded)	4 May, ,,
Lt. F. E. Beauchamp	8 Aug., ,,
2nd-Lt. E. P. Larrabee (wounded)	20 Sept., ,,

DECORATIONS
WON IN No. 24 SQUADRON, R.A.F.

DISTINGUISHED SERVICE ORDER.

1916.

Captain A. M. Wilkinson.
Lieut. P. A. Langan Byrne.
2nd-Lieut. A. G. Knight.
2nd-Lieut. H. C. Evans.

1917.

Captain S. H. Long.

1918.

Captain T. F. Hazell.

BAR TO D.S.O.

1916.

Captain A. M. Wilkinson.

MILITARY CROSS.

1916.

2nd-Lieut. D. M. Tidmarsh.
2nd-Lieut. S. E. Cowan.
2nd-Lieut. W. A. C. Morgan.
2nd-Lieut. A. G. Knight.
Lieut. D. Wilson.
Captain J. O. Andrews.
Lieut. C. M. B. Chapman

1917.

Captain R. H. M. S. Saundby.
Captain H. W. Woollett.
Captain B. P. G. Beanlands.

1918.

2nd-Lieut. A. K. Cowper.
2nd-Lieut. H. B. Richardson.
Captain A. J. Brown.
2nd-Lieut. H. B. Redler.
2nd-Lieut. R. T. Mark.
Captain. I. D. R. Macdonald.
Captain C. N. Lowe.

BAR TO MILITARY CROSS.

1916.

2nd-Lieut. S. E. Cowan.
Captain J. O. Andrews.

1918.

Captain A. K. Cowper.
2nd-Lieut. R. T. Mark.

2nd BAR TO MILITARY CROSS.

1916.

Captain J. O. Andrews.
2nd-Lieut. S. E. Cowan.

1918.

Captain A. K. Cowper.
Captain G. E. H. McElroy.

DISTINGUISHED FLYING CROSS.

1918.

2nd-Lieut. P. J. Nolan.
Captain I. D. R. MacDonald.
Lieut. J. A. E. R. Daley.
Captain C. N. Lowe.
Lieut. W. C. Lambert.
Captain T. F. Hazell.
Lieut. H. D. Barton.
Lieut. G. B. Foster.
Captain W. Selwyn.
Lieut. C. M. G. Farrell.
2nd-Lieut. H. L. Bair.
2nd-Lieut. T. M. Harries.

BAR TO DISTINGUISHED FLYING CROSS.

1918.

Captain T. F. Hazell.
Captain H. D. Barton.
Captain W. H. Longton.

2nd BAR TO DISTINGUISHED FLYING CROSS.

1918.

Captain W. H. Longton.

MERITORIOUS SERVICE MEDAL.

1916.

Tech. Sergt.-Major J. R. Gardiner, No. 178.

1918.

Tech.-Sergt.-Major Schofield, F., No. 5974.
Flight Sergt. Fisher, A.J., No. 10589.

To be Brevet-Major.

1917.

Capt. (temp. Maj.) C. E. C. Rabagliati, M.C.

MENTIONED IN DESPATCHES.

1916.

Captain E. H. Mitchell.
Captain J. O. Andrews (3).
Captain A. M. Wilkinson.
Lieut. A. G. Knight.
2nd-Lieut. H. C. Evans.

1917.

Captain S. H. Long.

1918.

Major V. A. H. Robeson.
Captain J. Palmer.
Lieut. C. A. Bissonnette.
2nd-Lieut. P. Brindle.
Sergeant G. T. Haines, No. 6200

CROIX DE GUERRE AVEC PALME.

1918.

Lieut. R. G. Hammersley.

CROIX DE GUERRE AVEC ETOILE BRONZE.

1918.

Major V. A. H. Robeson.
Captain G. O. Johnson.

PART IV.

SUMMARY OF DECISIVE FIGHTING.

Machine in use.	De H.2.	De H.5.	S.E. 5a.	Totals.
Dates	8 April, 1916, to 25 May, 1917.	25 May, 1917, to 25 Dec., 1917.	25 Dec. 1917, to 11 Nov., 1918.	—
Number of Combats	774	205	783	1762
Enemy Machines completely destroyed or captured	44	3	108, & 20 balloons	175
Enemy Machines driven down out of control (confirmed)	2	5	25	32
Enemy Machines driven down out of control (unconfirmed)	26	12	52	90
Total number of Enemy Machines accounted for				297

SUMMARY OF INDECISIVE FIGHTING.

Machine in use.	De H.2.	De H.5.	S.E. 5a.	Totals.
Enemy Machines forced to land in their own lines	17	2	12	31
Enemy Machines driven down damaged or possibly out of control	28	4	44	76
Enemy Observers reported hit	12	—	25	37
Enemy Machines driven down out of reach	100	14	136	250

SUMMARY OF LOW-FLYING WORK.

Date.	Bombs dropped. (25 lbs.).	Rounds fired.	Reconnaisances.	Machine in use.
1917, August	—	4,550	—	D.H. 5
,, September	—	250	—	
,, October	—	50	—	
,, November	4	650	—	
,, December	44	2,550	—	
1918, February	—	300	—	S.E. 5A
,, March	637	25,405	14	
,, April	307	7,765	45	
,, May	36	50	8	
,, June	—	—	16	
,, July	204	8,260	28	
,, August	348	15,507	102	
,, September	306	5,400	53	
,, October	312	20,260	71	
,, November	79	9,775	23	
Total	2,277	100,572	360	

DETAILS OF DECISIVE COMBATS.

Date. 1916.	Pilot's Name.	Fate of Enemy.	Remarks. Type of Machine in use.
April 2 ...	2nd-Lieut. D. M. Tidmarsh, M.C.	Crashed & burnt.	De H. 2.
,, 2 ...	2nd-Lieut. S. J. Sibley	(Crashed & burnt.)	
,, 30 ...	2nd-Lieut. D. M. Tidmarsh, M.C.	Crashed.	
May 4 ...	2nd-Lieut. S. E. Cowan, M.C.	Crashed.	
,, 16 ...	Captain A. M. Wilkinson, D.S.O.	Out of control.	
,, 16 ...	Captain A. M. Wilkinson, D.S.O.	Out of control.	
,, 20 ...	2nd-Lieut. D. M. Tidmarsh, M.C.	In flames.	
,, 20 ...	2nd-Lieut. D. Wilson, M.C.	Crashed & burnt.	
June 17 ...	Lieut. H. D. Gray	Crashed.	
,, 18 ...	2nd-Lieut. W. A. C. Morgan, M.C.	Captured.	Intact.
,, 18 ...	Captain A. M. Wilkinson, D.S.O.	Crashed.	
,, 18 ...	2nd-Lieut. C. Kerr	Out of control.	
,, 22 ...	Lieut. C. M. B. Chapman, M.C.	Crashed.	
,, 25 ...	Lieut. N. P. Manfield	Broken in air.	
July 1 ...	2nd-Lieut. S. E. Cowan, M.C.	Crashed.	
,, 1 ...	2nd-Lieut. S. E. Cowan, M.C.	Crashed.	
,, 6 ...	2nd-Lieut. H. A. Wood	Crashed.	
,, 9 ...	2nd-Lieut. F. W. Honnet	Crashed.	
,, 9 ...	2nd-Lieut. S. E. Pither	Out of control.	
,, 10 ...	2nd-Lieut. P. B. Prothero	Crashed.	(Bristol Scout [used)
,, 14 ...	Lieut. C. M. B. Chapman, M.C.	Out of control.	
,, 19 ...	2nd-Lieut. D. Wilson, M.C.	Out of control.	
,, 19 ...	Lieut. A. G. Knight, D.S.O., M.C.	Out of control.	
,, 20 ...	2nd-Lieut. H. E. Evans, D.S.O.	Out of control.	
,, 20 ...	Lieut. C. M. B. Chapman, M.C.	Crashed.	
,, 20 ...	2nd-Lieut. A. E. McKay	Out of control.	
,, 21 ...	Captain J. O. Andrews, D.S.O., M.C.	Crashed.	
,, 21 ...	Sergeant W. Piercey	Crashed.	
,, 29 ...	2nd-Lieut. S. E. Cowan, M.C.	Crashed.	
,, 31 ...	2nd-Lieut. R. H. M. S. Saundby, M.C.	Out of control.	Confirmed.
Aug. 3 ...	2nd-Lieut. S. E. Cowan, M.C.	Out of control.	
,, 3 ...	2nd-Lieut. A. E. Glew	Out of control.	
,, 6 ...	2nd-Lieut. H. C. Evans, D.S.O.	Out of control.	Confirmed.
,, 7 ...	2nd-Lieut. E. R. Yates	Out of control.	
,, 9 ...	2nd-Lieut. A. E. Glew	Out of control.	
,, 9 ...	Captain J. O. Andrews, D.S.O., M.C.	Out of control.	
,, 21 ...	2nd-Lieut. S. J. Sibley	Crashed.	
,, 29 ...	2nd-Lieut. A. E. Glew	Out of control.	
,, 31 ...	Captain A. M. Wilkinson, D.S.O.	Out of control.	
,, 31 ...	Captain A. M. Wilkinson, D.S.O.	Crashed.	
Sept. 2 ..	Captain J. O. Andrews, D.S.O., M.C.	Crashed.	
,, 14 ...	2nd-Lieut. A. G. Knight, D.S.O., M.C.	In flames.	
,, 15 ...	2nd-Lieut. P. A. Langan Byrne, D.S.O.	In flames.	
,, 15 ...	2nd-Lieut. A. G. Knight, D.S.O., M.C.	In flames.	
,, 16 ...	2nd-Lieut. S. E. Cowan, MC..	In flames.	
Oct. 17 ...	2nd-Lieut. A. G. Knight, D.S.O., M.C.	Out of control.	
,, 20 ...	Lieut. H. A. Wood	Crashed.	
,, 21 ...	2nd-Lieut. J. H. Crutch	Out of control.	
,, 26 ...	2nd-Lieut. K. Crawford	Out of control.	
Nov. 3 ...	2nd-Lieut. E. C. Pashley	Out of control.	
,, 9 ...	2nd-Lieut. E. C. Pashley	Destroyed.	
,, 16 ...	2nd-Lieut. H. A. Wood	Out of control.	
,, 16 ...	Captain S. H. Long, D.S.O., M.C.	Crashed.	
,, 16 ...	2nd-Lieut. E. C. Pashley	Out of control.	
,, 17 ...	Captain J. O. Andrews, D.S.O., M.C.	In flames.	
,, 22 ...	Captain J. O. Andrews, D.S.O., M.C.	Crashed.	
,, 22 ...	2nd-Lieut. E. C. Pashley	Crashed.	
,, 22 ...	2nd-Lieut. K. Crawford	Crashed.	
Dec. 11 ...	2nd-Lieut. E. C. Pashley	Crashed & burnt.	

Date.	Pilot's Name.	Fate of Enemy.	Remarks. Type of Machine in use
1917.			
Jan. 23 ...	2nd-Lieut. E. C. Pashley	Pilot fell out.	De H. 2.
,, 24 ...	Captain H. A. Wood	Forced to land our side.	
,, 25 ...	2nd-Lieut. A. E. McKay	Do. do.	
,, 25 ...	Captain S. H. Long, D.S.O., M.C.	In flames.	
,, 25 ...	2nd-Lieut. A. E. McKay	Crashed.	
,, 27 ...	Captain S. H. Long, D.S.O., M.C.	Crashed.	
Feb. 4 ...	2nd-Lieut. E. C. Pashley	Crashed.	
,, 6 ...	2nd-Lieut. S. Cockerell	Out of control.	
April 2 ...	2nd-Lieut. S. Cockerell	Crashed.	
,, 2 ...	2nd-Lieut. A. K. Crawford	In flames.	
,, 5 ...	2nd-Lieut. H. W. Woollett, D.S.O., M.C.	Crashed.	
,, 6 ...	Lieuts. C. R. Keary & T. C. Arnot	Out of control.	
May 10 ...	Lieut. A. K. Crawford	Out of control.	
,, 25 ...	2nd -Lieut S. Cockerell	Crashed.	De H. 5.
July 23 ...	Captain W. H. Woollett, D.S.O., M.C.	Crashed.	
,, 24 ...	2nd-Lieut. B. L. Blofeld	Out of control.	
,, 28 ...	Captain W. H. Woollett, D.S.O., M.C.	Out of control.	Confirmed.
Aug. 17 ...	Captain W. H. Woollett, D.S.O., M.C.	Out of control.	
,, 25 ...	Captain B. P. G. Beanlands, M.C.	Out of control.	Confirmed.
Oct. 21 ...	2nd-Lieut. R. C. Davies	Out of control.	
Nov. 9 ...	2nd-Lieut. A. K. Cowper, M.C.	Out of control.	
,, 13 ...	2nd-Lieut. A. K. Cowper, M.C.	Out of control.	
,, 13 ...	Captain B. P. G. Beanlands, M.C.	Out of control.	Confirmed.
,, 13 ...	Captain B. P. G. Beanlands, M.C.	Out of control.	Confirmed.
,, 15 ...	2nd-Lieut. I. D. R. McDonald, M.C. D.F.C. ...	Out of control.	
,, 15 ...	2nd-Lieut. J. H. Jephson	Out of control.	
,, 15 ...	2nd-Lieut. I. D. R. McDonald, M.C., D.F.C. ...	Out of control.	Confirmed.
,, 30 ...	2nd-Lieut. J. W. Jackson	Out of control.	
,, 30 ...	2nd-Lieut. I. D. R. McDonald, M.C., D.F.C. ...	Out of control.	
,, 30 ...	Captain B. P. G. Beanlands, M.C.	Out of control.	
Dec. 10 ...	Captain A. J. Brown, M.C.	Out of control.	
Dec. 10 ...	2nd-Lieut. E. G. Johnston	Out of control.	
,, 10 ...	2nd-Lieut. I. D. R. McDonald, M.C., D.F.C. ...	Crashed.	
1918.			
Feb. 16 ...	Captain J. C. Ralston, M.C.	Out of control.	S.E. 5A.
,, 18 ...	2nd-Lieut. A. K. Cowper, M.C. 2nd-Lieut. H. D. Barton, D.F.C. 2nd-Lieut. R. T. Mark, M.C.	Out of control.	
,, 18 ...	2nd-Lieut. A. K. Cowper, M.C.	Out of control.	
,, 18 ...	2nd-Lieut. R. T. Mark, M.C.	Out of control.	
,, 18 ...	2nd-Lieut. H. B. Richardson, M.C.	Out of control.	
,, 19 ...	2nd-Lieut. A. K. Cowper, M.C. 2nd-Lieut. P. A. McDougall, M.C. 2nd-Lieut. R. T. Mark, M.C. 2nd-Lieut. R. G. Hammersley	Crashed.	
,, 19 ...	2nd-Lieut. A. K. Cowper, M.C. 2nd-Lieut. P. A. McDougall, M.C. 2nd-Lieut. R. T. Mark, M.C. 2nd-Lieut. R. G. Hammersley	In flames.	
,, 21 ...	Captain G. E. H. McElroy, D.S.O., M.C., D.F.C.	Out of control.	Confirmed.
,, 21 ...	2nd-Lieut. P. A. McDougall, M.C.	Out of control.	
,, 26 ...	2nd-Lieut. A. K. Cowper, M.C.	Captured intact.	
,, 26 ...	2nd-Lieut. A. K. Cowper, M.C.	Broke up in air.	
,, 26 ...	2nd-Lieut. I. D. R. McDonald, M.C., D.F.C. ...	Crashed.	
,, 26 ...	Captain G. E. H. McElroy, D.S.O., M.C., D.F.C.	In flames.	
,, 26 ...	2nd-Lieut. P. A. McDougall, M.C.	Crashed.	
,, 26 ...	2nd-Lieut. H. B. Richardson, M.C.	Out of control.	
,, 26 ...	2nd-Lieut. R. G. Hammersley	Out of control.	
,, 27 ...	Captain S. H. Long, D.S.O., M.C.	Out of control.	

Date.	Pilot's Name.	Fate of Enemy.	Remarks. Type of Machine in use
1918.			
Feb. 26 ...	2nd-Lieut. I. D. R. McDonald, M.C., D.F.C. ...	Crashed.	
	2nd-Lieut. J. J. Dawe		
	2nd-Lieut. H. V. L. Tubbs		
	2nd-Lieut. R. T. Mark, M.C.		
	2nd-Lieut. H. B. Richardson, M.C.		
	2nd-Lieut. W. F. Poulter		
Mar. 1 ...	Captain G. E. H. McElroy, D.S.O., M.C., D.F.C.	Out of control.	
,, 6 ...	Captain G. E. H. McElroy, D.S.O., M.C., D.F.C.	Crashed.	
,, 6 ...	2nd-Lieut. H. B. Richardson, M.C.	Crashed.	
,, 6 ...	Captain A. J. Brown, M.C.	Crashed.	
	2nd-Lieut. A. K. Cowper, M.C.		Confirmed.
,, 6 ...	2nd-Lieut. J. J. Dawe	Out of control.	Confirmed.
,, 6 ...	Captain G. E. H. McElroy, D.S.O., M.C., D.F.C.	In flames.	
,, 6 ...	2nd-Lieut. P. A. McDougall, M.C.	Out of control.	
,, 6 ...	Lieut. R. G. Hammersley	Out of control.	
,, 6 ...	2nd-Lieut. D. M. Clementz	Crashed.	
,, 8 ...	2nd-Lieut. A. K. Cowper, M.C.	Crashed.	
,, 8 ...	Captain G. E. H. McElroy, D.S.O., M.C., D.F.C.	Out of control.	
,, 8 ...	Captain G. E. H. McElroy, D.S.O., M.C., D.F.C.	Crashed.	
,, 8 ...	2nd-Lieut. H. D. Barton, D.F.C.	In flames.	
,, 9 ...	Captain G. E. H. McElroy, D.S.O., M.C., D.F.C.	Out of control.	Confirmed.
,, 9 ...	2nd-Lieut. H. V. L. Tubbs	Out of control.	Confirmed.
,, 11 ...	Captain A. J. Brown, M.C.	Out of control.	Confirmed.
	2nd-Lieut. P. J. Nolan, M.C.		
	2nd-Lieut. R. T. Mark, M.C.		
	2nd-Lieut. H. B. Richardson, M.C.		
	2nd-Lieut. E. W. Lindeburg		
	2nd-Lieut. R. G. Hammersley		
,, 11 ...	Captain A. J. Brown, M.C.	Out of control.	
,, 11 ...	2nd-Lieut. H. B. Richardson, M.C.	Out of control.	
,, 11 ...	2nd-Lieut. H. D. Barton, D.F.C.	Out of control.	
,, 12 ...	2nd-Lieut. H. V. L. Tubbs	Out of control.	Confirmed.
,, 12 ...	2nd-Lieut. J. J. Dawe	Out of control.	Confirmed.
,, 12 ...	2nd-Lieut. I. D. R. McDonald, M.C., D.F.C. ...	Crashed.	
,, 12 ...	Captain A. J. Brown, M.C.	Crashed.	Confirmed.
,, 13 ...	2nd-Lieut. A. K. Cowper, M.C.	Out of control.	
,, 13 ...	Captain A. J. Brown, M.C.	Out of control.	
,, 13 ...	2nd-Lieut. R. T. Mark, M.C.	Out of control.	
,, 15 ...	2nd-Lieut. A. K. Cowper, M.C.	Crashed.	
	2nd-Lieut. R. T. Mark, M.C.		
	2nd-Lieut. H. B. Richardson, M.C.		
,, 15 ...	2nd-Lieut. H. B. Redler, M.C.	Out of control.	
,, 16 ...	2nd-Lieut. H. B. Richardson, M.C.	Crashed.	
,, 16 ...	2nd-Lieut. J. J. Dawe	Out of control.	
	2nd-Lieut. H. V. L. Tubbs		
,, 17 ...	2nd-Lieut. A. K. Cowper, M.C.	Crashed.	Confirmed.
,, 17 ...	2nd-Lieut. H. B. Richardson, M.C.	Out of control.	Confirmed.
,, 18 ...	Captain B. P. G. Beanlands, M.C.	Out of control.	
	2nd-Lieut. H. B. Redler, M.C.		
,, 18 ...	Lieut. A. K. Cowper, M.C.	Out of control.	
21 ...	2nd-Lieut. H. B. Richardson, M.C.	Out of control.	
,, 21 ...	2nd-Lieut. H. B. Richardson, M.C.	Out of control.	
,, 21 ...	2nd-Lieut. H. B. Richardson, M.C.	Crashed.	
,, 21 ...	Lieut. A. K. Cowper, M.C.	Out of control.	
,, 21 ...	Lieut. A. K. Cowper, M.C.	In flames.	
,, 21 ...	2nd-Lieut. P. J. Nolan, D.F.C.	Out of control.	
,, 22 ...	2nd-Lieut. R. T. Mark, M.C.	In flames.	Confirmed.
,, 22 ...	2nd-Lieut. H. B. Richardson, M.C.	Crashed.	
,, 22 ...	2nd-Lieut. P. J. Nolan, D.F.C.	Assisted in destruction of 3 E.A.	
,, 23 ...	Lieut. A. K. Cowper, M.C.	Crashed.	
,, 23 ...	2nd-Lieut. H. B. Redler, M.C.	Crashed.	
,, 23 ...	Lieut. A. K. Cowper, M.C.	Crashed.	
	2nd-Lieut. P. J. Nolan, D.F.C.		
	2nd-Lieut. C M. G. Farrell, D.F.C.		
,, 23 ...	2nd-Lieut. R. G. Hammersley	Out of control.	Confirmed.
,, 24 ...	2nd-Lieut. H. B. Redler, M.C.	Crashed.	

Date.	Pilot's Name.	Fate of Enemy.	Remarks. Type of Machine in use.
1918.			
Mar. 24 ...	2nd-Lieut. E. W. Lindeberg	Crashed.	
,, 26 ...	2nd-Lieut. H. B. Redler, M.C.	Crashed.	
,, 26 ...	2nd-Lieut. H. B. Richardson, M.C.	Crashed.	
,, 26 ...	2nd-Lieut. R. T. Mark, M.C.	Crashed.	
,, 26 ...	2nd-Lieut. J. A. E. R. Daley, D.F.C.	In flames.	
,, 27 ...	Captain G. E. H. McElroy, D.S.O., M.C., D.F.C.	Crashed.	
,, 29 ...	Captain A. K. Cowper, M.C.	Crashed.	
,, 29 ...	Captain G. E. H. McElroy, D.S.O., M.C., D.F.C.	Crashed.	
,, 29 ...	Captain G. E. H. McElroy, D.S.O., M.C., D.F.C.	Out of control.	
April 1 ...	Captain G. E. H. McElroy, D.S.O., M.C., D.F.C.	Crashed.	
,, 2 ...	Captain G. E. H. McElroy, D.S.O., M.C., D.F.C.	Out of control.	
,, 4 ...	2nd-Lieut. R. T. Mark, M.C. 2nd-Lieut. C. M. G. Farrell, D.F.C.	Crashed.	Confirmed.
,, 4 ...	2nd-Lieut. H. B. Richardson, M.C.	Crashed.	S.E. 5A Viper.
,, 4 ...	Captain G. E. H. McElroy, D.S.O., M.C., D.F.C.	Crashed.	
,, 7 ...	Captain I. D. R. McDonald, M.C., D.F.C.	Crashed.	
,, 7 ...	2nd-Lieut. W. C. Lambert, D.F.C.	Out of control.	
,, 7 ...	Captain G. E. H. McElroy, D.S.O., M.C., D.F.C.	Crashed.	
,, 7 ...	Captain G. E. H. McElroy, D.S.O., M.C., D.F.C.	Crashed.	
,, 7 ...	Captain G. E. H. McElroy, D.S.O., M.C., D.F.C.	Out of control.	
,, 10 ...	2nd-Lieut. J. J. Dawe	Out of control.	
,, 11 ...	Captain I. D. R. McDonald, M.C., D.F.C.	Out of control.	
,, 12 ...	2nd-Lieut. G. B. Foster, D.F.C.	Crashed.	
,, 12 ...	2nd-Lieut. H. B. Redler, M.C.	Crashed.	Confirmed.
,, 12 ...	Captain I. D. R. McDonald, M.C., D.F.C.	Crashed.	
,, 12 ...	Captain I. D. R. McDonald, M.C., D.F.C.	Out of control.	Confirmed.
,, 12 ...	2nd-Lieut. E. W. Lindeburg	Crashed.	Confirmed.
,, 12 ...	2nd-Lieut. J. J. Dawe	Crashed.	Confirmed.
,, 12 ...	2nd-Lieut. R. G. Hammersley	Crashed.	Confirmed.
,, 12 ...	2nd-Lieut. W. C. Lambert, D.F.C.	Crashed.	Confirmed.
,, 20 ...	Captain I. D. R. McDonald, M.C., D.F.C.	Crashed.	
,, 20 ...	2nd-Lieut. G. B. Foster, D.F.C.	Crashed.	
,, 20 ...	2nd-Lieut. H. B. Redler, M.C.	Out of control.	
,, 21 ...	Captain G. O. Johnson, M.C.	E.K.B. in flames.	
,, 23 ...	2nd-Lieut. R. T. Mark, M.C.	Crashed.	Confirmed.
,, 23 ...	Captain C. N. Lowe, M.C., D.F.C.	Out of control.	Confirmed.
,, 23 ...	Captain I. D. R. McDonald, M.C., D.F.C.	Crashed.	
,, 23 ...	Captain G. O. Johnson, M.C.	Crashed.	Confirmed.
May 3 ...	Captain C. N. Lowe, M.C., D.F.C. Lieut. R. T. Mark, M.C.	Out of control.	
,, 3 ...	Captain I. D. R. McDonald, M.C., D.F.C.	Crashed.	
,, 4 ...	Captain G. O. Johnson, M.C.	Out of control.	
,, 4 ...	2nd-Lieut. W. C. Lambert, D.F.C.	Out of control.	
,, 9 ...	2nd-Lieut. J. A. E. R. Daley, D.F.C.	Crashed.	
,, 9 ...	2nd-Lieut. T. T. B. Hellet 2nd-Lieut. W. C. Lambert, D.F.C.	Crashed.	
,, 9 ...	Captain C. N. Lowe, M.C., D.F.C.	Out of control.	Confirmed.
,, 16 ...	2nd-Lieut. H. D. Barton, D.F.C.	Crashed.	
,, 16 ...	2nd-Lieut. C. M. G. Farrell, D.F.C.	Out of control.	Confirmed.
,, 16 ...	Captain I. D. R. McDonald, M.C., D.F.C.	Out of control.	Confirmed.
,, 19 ...	2nd-Lieut. R. G. Hammersley 2nd-Lieut. E. B. Wilson	Out of control.	
,, 20 ...	2nd-Lieut. J. Palmer	Out of control.	
,, 20 ...	2nd-Lieut. J. J. Dawe	Crashed.	
,, 20 ...	2nd-Lieut. R. G. Hammersley	Out of control.	
,, 20 ...	2nd-Lieut. W. C. Lambert; D.F.C.	Out of control.	
,, 20 ...	2nd-Lieut. J. A. E. R. Daley, D.F.C.	E.K.B. in flames.	
,, 28 ...	Captain I. D. R. McDonald, M.C., D.F.C.	Out of control.	Confirmed.
,, 31 ...	Captain I. D. R. McDonald, M.C., D.F.C.	Crashed.	Confirmed.
,, 31 ...	2nd-Lieut. J. J. Dawe	Crashed.	Confirmed.
June 2 ...	Captain I. D. R. McDonald, M.C., D.F.C.	Crashed.	Confirmed.
,, 2 ...	2nd-Lieut. J. A. E. R. Daley, D.F.C.	Crashed.	
,, 2 ...	2nd-Lieut. W. C. Lambert, D.F.C.	Crashed.	
,, 3 ...	Captain I. D. R. McDonald, M.C., D.F.C.	Crashed.	
,, 5 ...	Captain I. D. R. McDonald, M.C., D.F.C.	E.K.B. in flames.	

Date. 1918.	Pilot's Name.	Fate of Enemy.	Remarks. Type of Machine in use.
June 6 ...	Captain C. N. Lowe, M.C., D.F.C.	Crashed.	
,, 6 ...	2nd-Lieut. H. D. Barton, D.F.C.	Out of control.	
,, 6 ...	2nd-Lieut. E. W. Lindeburg	Out of control.	Confirmed.
,, 7 ...	Captain C. N. Lowe, M.C., D.F.C.	In flames.	
,, 7 ...	Captain I. D. R. McDonald, M.C., D.F.C.	Broke in air.	
,, 7 ...	2nd-Lieut. G. B. Foster, D.F.C.	Crashed.	
,, 7 ...	2nd-Lieut. E. B. Crossen	Out of control.	
,, 12 ...	Captain G. O. Johnson, M.C.	Out of control.	Confirmed.
,, 17 ...	Captain I. D. R. McDonald, M.C., D.F.C. Captain G. O. Johnson, M.C. 2nd-Lieut. H. D. Barton, D.F.C.	Captured.	Enemy pilot, Lt. Wüsthoff.
,, 17 ...	2nd-Lieut. W. C. Lambert, D.F.C.	In flames.	
,, 17 ...	2nd-Lieut. W. C. Lambert, D.F.C.	Broke in air.	
,, 25 ...	Captain C. N. Lowe, M.C., D.F.C.	In flames.	
,, 25 ...	2nd-Lieut. G. B. Foster, D.F.C.	Out of control.	
,, 27 ...	2nd-Lieut. H. D. Barton, D.F.C.	Out of control.	Confirmed.
,, 27 ...	2nd-Lieut. W. C. Lambert, D.F.C.	Out of control.	
,, 27 ...	2nd-Lieut. J. A. E. R. Daley, D.F.C.	Out of control.	
,, 29 ...	Captain W. Selwyn, D.F.C.	Out of control.	
,, 29 ...	2nd-Lieut. W. C. Lambert, D.F.C.	Crashed.	
,, 29 ...	2nd-Lieut. J. A. E. R. Daley, D.F.C.	In flames.	
July 1 ...	Captain C. N. Lowe, M.C., D.F.C. Lieut. H. D. Barton, D.F.C.	Out of control.	Confirmed.
,, 1 ...	2nd-Lieut. J. A. E. R. Daley, D.F.C.	E.K.B. in flames.	
,, 4 ...	Captain T. F. Hazell, D.S.O., M.C., D.F.C.	Out of control.	
,, 4 ...	2nd-Lieut. W. C. Lambert, D.F.C.	Crashed.	
,, 4 ...	2nd-Lieut. W. C. Lambert, D.F.C.	Crashed.	
,, 4 ...	Captain W. Selwyn, D.F.C.	Crashed.	
,, 16 ...	2nd-Lieut. H. D. Barton, D.F.C.	E.K.B. in flames.	Confirmed.
,, 17 ...	Captain T. F. Hazell, D.S.O., M.C., D.F.C.	E.K.B. in flames.	Confirmed.
,, 22 ...	Captain T. F. Hazell, D.S.O., M.C., D.F.C.	E.K.B. in flames.	
,, 23 ...	Captain T. F. Hazell, D.S.O., M.C., D.F.C. 2nd-Lieut. G. B. Foster, D.F.C.	E.K.B. deflated.	Confirmed as destroyed.
,, 26 ...	Captain T. F. Hazell, D.S.O., M.C., D.F.C.	E.K.B. in flames.	Confirmed.
,, 26 ...	Lieut. H. D. Barton, D.F.C. 2nd-Lieut. C. M. G. Farrell, D.F.C. 2nd-Lieut. J. Palmer 2nd-Lieut. F. S. Passmore 2nd-Lieut. W. J. Miller	Captured.	
,, 31 ...	Captain T. F. Hazell, D.S.O., M.C., D.F.C. 2nd-Lieut. G. B. Foster, D.F.C. 2nd-Lieut. E. P. Crossen	Crashed.	
Aug. 1 ...	Captain T. F. Hazell, D.S.O., M.C., D.F.C.	In flames.	Confirmed.
,, 4 ...	2nd-Lieut. H. D. Barton, D.F.C. 2nd-Lieut. C. M. G. Farrell, D.F.C.	Crashed.	
,, 4 ...	2nd-Lieut. C. M. G. Farrell, D.F.C.	Out of control.	
,, 4 ...	2nd-Lieut. W. C. Lambert, D.F.C.	Crashed.	
,, 8 ...	2nd-Lieut. W. C. Lambert, D.F.C.	E.K.B. deflated.	
,, 8 ...	2nd-Lieut. T. M. Harries, D.F.C.	Crashed.	
,, 8 ...	Captain T. F. Hazell, D.S.O., M.C., D.F.C.	Out of control.	Confirmed.
,, 8 ...	Captain T. F. Hazell, D.S.O., M.C., D.F.C.	Broke in air.	
,, 8 ...	Captain T. F. Hazell, D.S.O., M.C., D.F.C.	Captured.	
,, 10 ...	Captain W. Selwyn, D.F.C. 2nd-Lieut. W. C. Lambert, D.F.C. 2nd-Lieut. T. M. Harries, D.F.C. 2nd-Lieut. H. L. Bair, D.F.C. (U.S.A.S.)	Out of control.	
,, 10 ...	Captain T. F. Hazell, D.S.O., M.C., D.F.C. 2nd-Lieut. J. H. Southey	Out of control.	
,, 10 ...	C. M. G. Farrell, D.F.C.	Crashed.	
,, 10 ...	2nd-Lieut. W. C. Lambert, D.F.C.	Out of control.	
,, 10 ...	2nd-Lieut. W. C. Lambert, D.F.C.	Crashed.	
,, 10 ...	2nd-Lieut. G. B. Foster, D.F.C.	In flames.	
,, 10 ...	Captain T. F. Hazell, D.S.O., M.C., D.F.C.	In flames.	Confirmed.
,, 14 ...	Captain T. F. Hazell, D.S.O., M.C., D.F.C.	Out of control.	Confirmed.
,, 19 ...	Captain W. Selwyn, D.F.C.	Out of control.	Confirmed.
,, 19 ...	2nd-Lieut. T. M. Harries, D.F.C.	Out of control.	

Date.	Pilot's Name.	Fate of Enemy.	Remarks. Type of Machine in use.
1918.			
Aug. 19 ...	2nd-Lieut. H. L. Bair, D.F.C. (U.S. A.S.)	Out of control.	Confirmed.
,, 21 ...	Captain T. F. Hazell, D.S.O., M.C., D.F.C. ... 2nd-Lieut. H. Southey	E.K.B. deflated.	Confirmed.
,, 21 ...	Captain T. F. Hazell, D.S.O., M.C., D.F.C. ...	E.K.B. in flames.	Confirmed.
,, 22 ...	Captain T. F. Hazell, D.S.O., M.C., D.F.C. ...	E.K.B. in flames.	
,, 28 ...	Captain H. D. Barton, D.F.C.	Crashed.	
,, 30 ...	Captain H. D. Barton, D.F.C. .... 2nd-Lieut. H. L. Bair, D.F.C. (U.S. A.S.) .... 2nd-Lieut. T. M. Harries, D.F.C.	Crashed.	Confirmed.
Sept. 4 ...	Captain T. F. Hazell, D.S.O., M.C., D.F.C. ...	E.K.B. in flames.	Confirmed.
,, 4 ...	Captain T. F. Hazell, D.S.O., M.C., D.F.C. ...	E.K.B. & Winch in flames.	Confirmed.
,, 4 ...	2nd-Lieut. J. H. Southey	E.K.B. deflated.	
,, 4 ...	2nd-Lieut. E. P. Crossen	E.K.B. Observer in parachute.	Crashed.
,, 8 ...	Captain T. F. Hazell, D.S.O., M.C., D.F.C. ...	Crashed.	
,, 8 ...	2nd-Lieut. H. L. Bair, D.F.C. (U.S. A.S.)	Crashed.	
,, 8 ...	Captain H. D. Barton, D.F.C.	Out of control.	
,, 15 ...	Captain H. D. Barton, D.F.C.	Out of control.	Confirmed.
,, 15 ...	Captain H. D. Barton, D.F.C. .... 2nd-Lieut. H. L. Bair, D.F.C. (U.S. A.S.)	Crashed.	
,, 20 ...	Captain H. D. Barton, D.F.C.	Crashed.	
,, 22 ...	Captain H. D. Barton, D.F.C.	Crashed.	
Oct. 2 ...	Captain T. F. Hazell, D.S.O., M.C., D.F.C. ...	E.K.B. in flames.	
,, 2 ...	2nd-Lieut. W. C. Sterling	E.K.B. in flames.	
,, 2 ...	Captain H. D. Barton, D.F.C. .... 2nd-Lieut. W. G. C. Geraghty	E.K.B. in flames.	
,, 4 ...	Captain T. F. Hazell, D.S.O., M.C., D.F.C. ...	Crashed.	Confirmed.
,, 4 ...	Captain T. F. Hazell, D.S.O., M.C., D.F.C. ...	Crashed.	Confirmed.
,, 8 ...	Captain W. H. Longton, D.F.C., A.F.C.	E.K.B. in flames.	
,, 14 ...	Captain W. H. Longton, D.F.C., A.F.C.	Crashed.	
,, 25 ...	2nd-Lieut. W. G. C. Geraghty	Crashed.	
,, 29 ...	Captain W. H. Longton, D.F.C., A.F.C.	Crashed.	
,, 29 ...	Captain J. Palmer	Crashed.	
,, 29 ...	Captain W. H. Longton, D.F.C., A.F.C. .... 2nd-Lieut. T. M. Harries, D.F.C. .... 2nd-Lieut. H. V. Evans	Crashed.	Confirmed.
,, 30 ...	Captain W. H. Longton, D.F.C., A.F.C.	Crashed.	

In addition evidence of decisive combats as follows has been found, but as no official record is available, they have not been included :—

Date	Pilot's Name	Fate of Enemy	Source
1916.			
June 17 ...	Captain Wilkinson, D.S.O.	Crashed.	Diary of No. 5514 Sergeant Percy, No. 24 Squadron, R.A.F.
,, 30 ...	Lieut. Prothero	Crashed.	
July 31 ...	Sergeant Piercy	Brought down.	
Aug. 8 ...	Lieut. Evans, D.S.O.	Crashed.	
,, 22 ...	Lieut. Sibley	Crashed.	
Sept. 2 ...	Captain Andrews, D.S.O., M.C.	Crashed.	
1917.			
Feb. 7 ...	Lieut. Pashley	Crashed.	Diary of Sir W. E. Jaffray, Bart., R.O., No. 24 Squadron, R.A.F.
April 5 ...	Lieut. Cockerell	Crashed.	
,, 5 ...	Lieut. Crawford	In flames.	
,, 6 ...	Captain Woollett, D.S.O., M.C.	Crashed.	
May 25 ...	Lieut. Cockerell	Crashed.	

In addition, in Sir W. E. Jaffray's diary the following combats are labelled "Decisive, Out of Control," but as no official decision is available, they have been counted as "Driven down."

1917.
July 22 ... Lieut. White ....
,, 23 ... Captain Woollett, D.S.O., M.C. ....

DETAILS OF INDECISIVE COMBATS.

Date.	Pilot's Name.	Fate of Enemy.	Remarks. Type of Machine in use.
1916.			
June 10 ...	2nd-Lieut. W. A. C. Morgan, M.C.	Forced to land.	De H. 2.
,, 18 ...	Captain A. M. Wilkinson, D.S.O.	Forced to land.	
,, 18 ...	Captain A. M. Wilkinson, D.S.O.	Forced to land.	
,, 18 ...	2nd-Lieut. W. A. C. Morgan, M.C.	Forced to land.	
,, 23 ...	2nd-Lieut. K. H. A. Elliot	Forced to land.	
July 1 ...	2nd-Lieut. S. E. Cowan, M.C.	Observer apparently hit.	
,, 1 ...	2nd-Lieut. T. H. Bayetto	Forced to land.	M/C. Mor-
,, 29 ...	Captain J. O. Andrews, D.S.O., M.C.	Driven down damaged.	[aneBullet.
,, 30 ...	Lieut. C. M. B. Chapman, M.C.	Observer apparently hit.	
Aug. 8 ...	Captain J. O. Andrews, D.S.O., M.C.	Observer apparently hit.	
,, 21 ...	2nd-Lieut. S. J. Sibley	Observer apparently hit.	
,, 25 ...	Captain A. M. Wilkinson, D.S.O.	Observer apparently hit.	
,, 31 ...	Lieut. P. A. Langan Byrne, D.S.O.	Forced to land.	
Sept. 6 ...	Captain A. M. Wilkinson, D.S.O.	Observer apparently hit.	
,, 6 ...	2nd-Lieut. R. H. M. S. Saundby, M.C.	Driven down damaged.	
,, 7 ...	Lieut. N. P. Manfield	Driven down damaged.	
,, 7 ...	Captain D. M. Tidmarsh, M.C.	Driven down damaged.	
,, 7 ...	2nd-Lieut. H. A. Wood	Driven down damaged and observer hit.	
,, 16 ...	2nd-Lieut. S. E. Cowan, M.C.	Driven down damaged.	
,, 21 ...	Lieut. P. A. Langan Byrne, D.S.O.	Forced to land.	
,, 22 ...	Captain J. O. Andrews, D.S.O., M.C.	Driven down damaged.	
,, 22 ...	Lieut. P. A. Langan Byrne, D.S.O.	Forced to land.	
,, 22 ...	Lieut. P. A. Langan Byrne, D.S.O.	Forced to land.	
,, 23 ...	Lieut. P. A. Langan Byrne, D.S.O.	Forced to land & Pilot apparently hit.	
,, 28 ...	2nd-Lieut. A. G. Knight, D.S.O., M.C.	Observer apparently hit.	
,, 28 ...	Lieut. P. A. Langan Byrne, D.S.O.	Forced to land.	
,, 30 ...	Captain J. O. Andrews, D.S.O., M.C.	Driven down damaged.	
Oct. 16 ...	Lieut. P. A. Langan Byrne, D.S.O.	Forced to land.	
,, 20 ...	Lieut. A. G. Knight, D.S.O., M.C.	Driven down damaged.	
,, 21 ...	Captain J. O. Andrews, D.S.O., M.C.	Driven down damaged.	
,, 21 ...	Captain J. O. Andrews, D.S.O., M.C.	Driven down damaged.	
,, 26 ...	Lieut. E. C. Pashley	Forced to land.	
,, 26 ...	Lieut. E. Lewis	Forced to land.	
Nov. 2 ...	Captain J. O. Andrews, D.S.O., M.C.	Driven down damaged.	
,, 2 ...	Captain J. O. Andrews, D.S.O., M.C.	Driven down damaged.	
,, 3 ...	2nd-Lieut. A. E. McKay	Driven down damaged.	
,, 9 ...	Lieut. A. G. Knight, D.S.O., M.C.	Driven down damaged.	
,, 13 ...	2nd-Lieut. A. E. McKay	Driven down damaged.	
,, 16 ...	2nd-Lieut. A. E. McKay	Observer apparently hit.	
,, 16 ...	Captain J. O. Andrews, D.S.O., M.C.	Driven down damaged.	
,, 16 ...	2nd-Lieut. R. H. M. S. Saundby, M.C.	Driven down damaged.	
,, 17 ...	Captain J. O. Andrews, D.S.O., M.C.	Driven down damaged.	
,, 17 ...	Lieut. E. C. Pashley	Damaged.	
,, 17 ...	2nd-Lieut. H. B. Begg	Driven down damaged.	
,, 25 ...	2nd-Lieut. R. H. M. S. Saundby, M.C.	Driven down damaged.	
Dec. 20 ...	Captain S. H. Long, D.S.O., M.C.	Driven down damaged.	
,, 20 ...	Lieut. W. F. T. James	Driven down damaged.	
1917.			
Jan. 25 ...	Captain S. H. Long, D.S.O., M.C.	Driven down damaged and forced to land.	Confirmed.
Feb. 4 ...	Lieut. S. C. H. Begbie Lieut. S. Cockerell	Driven down damaged or out of control.	
,, 10 ...	2nd-Lieut. W. T. Hall	Forced to land and Observer apparently hit.	
Mar. 6 ...	Captain S. H. Long, D.S.O., M.C.	Observer apparently hit.	
,, 11 ...	Captain S. H. Long, D.S.O., M.C.	Driven down damaged.	

Date.	Pilot's Name.	Fate of Enemy.	Remarks. Type of Machine in use.
1917.			
May 2 ...	Lieut. S. Cockerell	Driven down damaged.	
,, 10 ...	2nd-Lieut. D. E. Evans	Driven down damaged.	
June 4 ...	Lieut. S. Cockerell	Forced to land.	
July 12 ...	2nd-Lieut. L. A. H. Terry	Driven down damaged.	
Aug. 25 ...	2nd-Lieut. W. B. Ives	Driven down damaged.	
Sept. 4 ...	Captain T. C. Arnot	Driven down damaged.	
,, 22 ...	Captain T. C. Arnot	Forced to land.	
,, 27 ...	2nd-Lieut. W. B. Ives	Driven down damaged.	
1918.			
Feb. 18 ...	2nd-Lieut. A. K. Cowper, M.C. 2nd-Lieut. H. D. Barton, D.F.C. 2nd-Lieut. R. T. Mark, M.C.	Observer apparently hit.	Viper, S.E. 5A.
,, 18 ...	2nd-Lieut. A. K. Cowper, M.C. 2nd-Lieut. H. D. Barton, D.F.C. 2nd-Lieut. R. T. Mark, M.C.	Damaged & Observer apparently hit.	
Mar. 1 ...	Lieut. H. V. L. Tubbs	Driven down damaged.	
,, 8 ...	Captain C. E. H. McElroy, D.S.O., M.C., D.F.C.	Observer apparently hit.	
,, 8 ...	2nd-Lieut. A. K. Cowper, M.C.	Driven down damaged.	
,, 12 ...	2nd-Lieut. H. B. Redler, M.C.	Observer apparently hit.	
,, 16 ...	2nd-Lieut. A. K. Cowper, M.C.	Observer apparently hit.	
,, 16 ...	Lieut. H. B. Richardson, M.C.	Observer apparently hit.	
,, 23 ...	2nd-Lieut. H. B. Redler, M.C.	Driven down damaged.	
,, 24 ...	2nd-Lieut. R. G. Hammersley 2nd-Lieut. W. Selwyn, D.F.C.	Observer apparently hit.	
April 4 ...	2nd-Lieut. E. T. Hendrie	Observer apparently hit.	
,, 10 ...	2nd-Lieut. E. T. Hendrie	Driven down damaged.	
,, 12 ...	2nd-Lieut. W. C. Lambert, D.F.C.	Driven down damaged and forced to land.	
,, 12 ...	2nd-Lieut. H. B. Redler, M.C.	Driven down damaged.	
,, 12 ... ,, 12 ...	2nd-Lieut. H. B. Redler, M.C. Captain I. D. R. McDonald, M.C., D.F.C.	Driven down damaged and forced to land.	
12 ...	2nd-Lieut. C. M. G. Farrell, D.F.C.	Observer apparently hit.	
,, 20 ...	2nd-Lieut. R. T. Mark, M.C.	Driven down damaged.	
,, 21 ...	2nd-Lieut. H. B. Redler, M.C.	Forced to land.	
May 9 ...	Captain C. N. Lowe, M.C., D.F.C.	Driven down damaged.	
,, 19 ...	2nd-Lieut. R. G. Hammersley	Driven down damaged.	
,, 19 ...	2nd-Lieut. R. T. Mark, M.C.	Forced to land.	
,, 20 ...	Captain C. N. Lowe, M.C., D.F.C.	Forced to land.	
,, 20 ...	2nd-Lieut. E. W. Lindeburg	Driven down damaged.	
,, 21 ...	2nd-Lieut. P. A. McDougall, M.C. Lieut. J. A. E. R. Daley, D.F.C. 2nd-Lieut. J. R. Hammersley Lieut. E. B. Wilson	Forced to land.	
,, 21 ...	2nd-Lieut. P. A. McDougall, M.C. 2nd-Lieut. J. J. Dawe Lieut. J. A. E. R. Daley, D.F.C.	Forced to land and Observer apparently hit.	
,, 31 ...	2nd-Lieut. P. A. McDougall, M.C. Lieut. E. B. Wilson 2nd-Lieut. J. J. Dawe 2nd-Lieut. J. H. Southey	Forced to land.	
June 1 ...	Lieut. W. C. Lambert, D.F.C.	Forced to land.	
,, 3 ...	Captain I. D. R. McDonald, M.C., D.F.C.	Observer apparently hit.	
,, 4 ...	Captain C. N. Lowe, M.C., D.F.C.	Observer apparently hit.	
,, 5 ...	Lieut. E. B. Wilson	Observer apparently hit.	
,, 5 ...	Lieut. E. B. Wilson	Driven down damaged.	
,, 5 ...	Lieut. G. B. Foster, D.F.C. Lieut. E. P. Crossen	Forced to land	
,, 6 ...	Captain C. N. Lowe, M.C., D.F.C. Lieut. E. B. Wilson	Driven down damaged.	

Date.	Pilots.	Fate of Enemy.	Remarks. Type of Machine in use.
1918.			
June 7 ...	Lieut. J. H. Southey	Driven down damaged.	
,, 14 ...	Lieut. W. C. Lambert, D.F.C.	Driven down damaged.	
,, 17 ...	Lieut. T. T. B. Hellett	Driven down damaged.	
,, 17 ...	Lieut. T. T. B. Hellett	Driven down damaged.	
,, 25 ...	Lieut. H. D. Barton, D.F.C. Lieut. J. H. Southey Lieut. E. B. Wilson Captain C. N. Lowe, M.C., D.F.C.	Driven down damaged.	
,, 26 ...	Lieut. J. A. E. R. Daley	Observer apparently hit.	
,, 26 ...	Captain W. Selwyn, D.F.C.	Observer apparently hit.	
,, 27 ...	Lieut. H. D. Barton, D.F.C. Lieut. F. S. Passmore Lieut. W. C. Lambert, D.F.C.	Driven down damaged.	
July 4 ...	Captain T. F. Hazell, D.S.O., M.C., D.F.C. 2nd-Lieut. H. D. Barton, D.F.C.	Driven down damaged.	
,, 4 ...	Lieut. G. B. Foster, D.F.C.	Driven down damaged.	
,, 4 ...	Lieut. G. M. G. Farrell, D.F.C.	Driven down damaged.	
,, 4 ...	Lieut. T. T. B. Hellett	Observer apparently hit.	
,, 4 ...	Lieut. W. C. Lambert, D.F.C.	Driven down damaged and forced to land.	
Aug. 7 ...	Lieut. W. C. Lambert, D.F.C.	Observer apparently hit.	
,, 8 ...	Lieut. R. K. Rose	Observer apparently hit.	
,, 8 ...	Captain T. F. Hazell, D.S.O., M.C., D.F.C.	Observer apparently hit.	
,, 9 ...	Captain W. Selwyn, D.F.C.	Observer apparently hit.	
,, 9 ...	Lieut. W. C. Lambert, D.F.C.	Driven down damaged.	
,, 14 ...	Lieut. H. L. Bair, D.F.C. (U.S. A.S.)	3 enemy driven down damaged.	
,, 16 ...	Lieut. W. C. Sterling	Observer apparently hit.	
,, 20 ...	Lieut. E. P. Crossen	Driven down damaged and forced to land.	
,, 21 ...	Captain T. F. Hazell, D.S.O., M.C., D.F.C.	Observer apparently hit.	
Sept. 2 ...	Captain W. Selwyn, D.F.C. 2nd-Lieut. T. M. Harries, D.F.C.	Driven down damaged.	
,, 2 ...	2nd-Lieut. T. M. Harries, D.F.C.	Observer apparently hit.	
,, 4 ...	Captain H. D. Barton, D.F.C.	Driven down damaged.	
,, 13 ...	Lieut. H. L. Bair, D.F.C. (U.S. A.S.)	Observer apparently hit.	
,, 16 ...	Lieut. W. C. Sterling Lieut. H. L. Bair, D.F.C. (U.S. A.S.) Lieut. R. K. Rose Captain H. D. Barton, D.F.C.	Driven down damaged.	
,, 18 ...	Captain H. D. Barton, D.F.C.	Observer apparently hit.	
,, 29 ...	Captain H. D. Barton, D.F.C.	Driven down damaged.	
Oct. 1 ...	Lieut. W. G. C. Geraghty	Observer's parachute damaged.	
,, 3 ...	2nd-Lieut. T. M. Harries, D.F.C.	Driven down damaged.	
,, 3 ...	Lieut. N. H. Barlow	Driven down damaged.	
,, 4 ...	Lieut. J. H. Southey	Driven down damaged.	
,, 4 ...	Lieut. E. P. Crossen	Driven down damaged.	
,, 8 ...	2nd-Lieut. T. M. Harries, D.F.C. Lieut. W. G. C. Geraghty	Driven down damaged.	
,, 8 ...	Lieut. N. H. Barlow		
,, 10 ...	2nd-Lieut. W. B. Thomson	Driven down damaged.	
,, 14 ...	2nd-Lieut. T. M. Harries, D.F.C.	Driven down damaged.	
,, 14 ...	Lieut. N. H. Barlow	Driven down damaged.	
,, 14 ...	Lieut. C. A. Bissonette	Driven down damaged.	
,, 29 ...	2nd-Lieut. H. V. Evans	Driven down damaged.	
,, 29 ...	Captain J. Palmer	Driven down damaged.	
,, 29 ...	Lieut. W. G. C. Geraghty	Driven down damaged.	
,, 29 ...	Lieut. N. H. Barlow	Driven down damaged.	
,, 30 ...	Lieut. N. H. Barlow	Driven down damaged.	

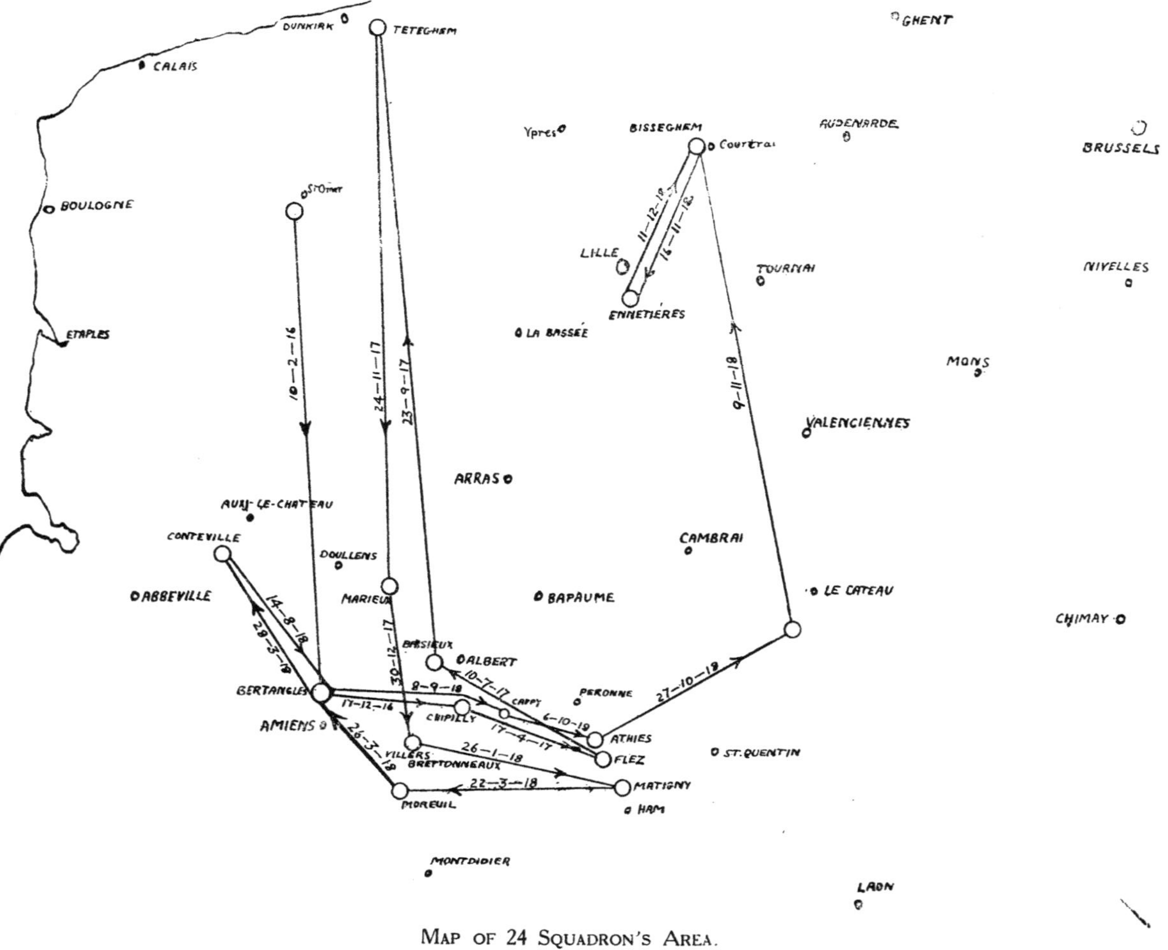

Map of 24 Squadron's Area.

A Table showing the movements of

No. 24 Squadron with the Wings and Brigades

it was attached to at each station.

Date	Event	Wing and Brigade
Sept. 1, 1915 ...	Squadron formed at Hounslow.	
Feb. 2, 1916 ...	M.T. left for B.E.F., France.	
,, 3, 1916 ...	M.T. arrived at Rouen.	
,, 6, 1916 ...	M.T. left Rouen for Abbeville.	
,, 6, 1916 ...	M.T. arrived at Abbeville.	
,, 7,, 1916 ...	M.T. left Abbeville for St. Omer.	
,, 7,, 1916 ...	M.T. arrived at St. Omer.	
,, 7,, 1916 ...	Machines arrived at St. Omer from England.	
,, 10, 1916 ...	Left St. Omer for Bertangles.	12th & 14th Wing, 4th Brigade
,, 10, 1916 ...	Arrived at Bertangles.	
Dec. 17, 1916 ...	Left for Chipilly.	
,, 17, 1916 ...	Arrived at Chipilly.	
April 17, 1917 ...	Left for Flez.	
,, 17, 1917 ...	Arrived at Flez.	
July 10, 1917 ...	Left for Baisieux.	
,, 10, 1917 ...	Arrived at Baisieux.	13th Wing, 3rd Brigade.
Sept. 23, 1917 ...	Left for Teteghem.	
,, 23, 1917 ...	Arrived at Teteghem.	14th Wing, 4th Brigade.
Nov. 24, 1917 ...	Left for Marieux.	
,, 24, 1917 ...	Arrived at Marieux.	13th Wing, 3rd Brigade.
Dec. 30, 1917 ...	Left for Villers Bretonneux.	
,, 30, 1917 ...	Arrived at Villers Bretonneux	22nd Wing, 5th Brigade.
Jan. 26, 1918 ...	Left for Matigny.	
,, 26, 1918 ...	Arrived at Matigny.	
Mar. 22, 1918 ...	Left for Moreuil.	
,, 22, 1918 ...	Arrived at Moreuil.	
,, 26, 1918 ...	Left for Bertangles.	
,, 26, 1918 ...	Arrived at Bertangles.	
,, 28, 1918 ...	Left for Conteville.	
,, 28, 1918 ...	Arrived at Conteville.	
Aug. 14, 1918 ...	Left for Bertangles.	
,, 14, 1918 ...	Arrived at Bertangles.	
Sept. 8, 1918 ...	Left for Cappy.	
,, 8, 1918 ...	Arrived at Cappy.	
Oct. 6, 1918 ...	Left for Athies.	
,, 6, 1918 ...	Arrived at Athies.	
,, 27, 1918 ...	Left for Busigny.	
,, 27, 1918 ...	Arrived at Busigny.	
Nov. 9, 1918 ...	Left for Bisseghem.	
,, 11, 1918 ...	Arrived at Bisseghem.	11th Wing, 2nd Brigade.
,, 16, 1918 ...	Left for Ennetiéres.	
,, 16, 1918 ...	Arrived at Ennetiéres.	80th Wing, 10th Brigade.
Dec. 11, 1918 ...	Left for Bisseghem.	
,, 11, 1918 ...	Arrived at Bisseghem.	65th Wing, 10th Brigade.
Jan. 22, 1919 ...	Machines handed back to depôt.	
Feb. 11, 1919 ...	Cadre left Bisseghem.	
12, 1919 ...	Cadre arrived at London Colney (England) via Boulogne.	

PART V.

ROLL OF OFFICERS.

SQUADRON COMMANDERS.

Captain A. G. Moore, M.C.	1st Sept., 1915, to 1st Oct., 1915.	
Major L. G. Hawker, V.C., D.S.O.	1st Oct., 1915, to 23rd Nov., 1916.	(K.)
†Major C. E. C. Rabagliati, M.C.	29th Nov., 1916, to 22nd Mar., 1917.	
Major A. G. Moore, M.C.	23rd Mar., 1917, to 24th Aug., 1917.	
Major J. G. Swart, M.C.	22nd Aug., 1917, to 1st Feb., 1918.	
Major V. A. H. Robeson, M.C.	1st Feb., 1918, to 3rd Feb., 1919.	

RECORDING OFFICERS.

2nd-Lieut. Sir W. E. Jaffray, Bart.	31st Dec., 1916, to 22nd Feb., 1918.
Lieut. G. M. Lindo	26th Mar., 1918, to 11th June, 1918.
Captain A. E. C. Lawson, M.C.	11th June, 1918, to 17th Sept., 1918.
Lieut. R. C. Allen	17th Sept., 1918, to 28th Oct., 1918.
Lieut. R. D. Bridgewater	30th Oct., 1918, to 17th Jan., 1919.
Lieut. R. C. Allen	17th Jan., 1919, to 3rd Feb., 1919.

EQUIPMENT OFFICERS.

Lieut. F. M. I. Watts	1st Nov., 1915, to 3rd Dec., 1916.
2nd-Lieut. J. Rigby	3rd Dec., 1916, to 24th May, 1917.
†Lieut. J. R. Frankish	22nd May, 1917, to 31st Oct., 1917.
†2nd-Lieut. H. T. H. Copeland	14th Nov., 1917, to 27th May, 1918.
2nd-Lieut. H. R. South	27th May, 1918 ,to 17th Sept., 1918.
2nd-Lieut. H. A. Young	28th Sept., 1918, to Cadre.

ARMAMENT OFFICERS.

2nd-Lieut. E. Y. Fitzgerald	20th June, 1917, to 27th Nov., 1917.
Lieut. O. G. Powell	24th Dec., 1917, to 4th Mar., 1918.
Lieut. E. W. Hallam	4th Mar., 1918. to 25th June, 1918.
2nd-Lieut. P. Brindle	11th July, 1918, to 3rd Feb., 1919.

ATTACHED OFFICERS.

Flying Officers :—

Lieut. F. E. Goodrich	18th June, 1916, to 10th July, 1916.	
Lieut. T. H. Bayetto	18th June, 1916, to 30th Aug., 1916.	(k.)
Lieut. T. B. Prothero	18th June, 1916, to 21st July, 1916.	(k.)
Lieut. C. H. Jenkins	18th June, 1916, to 30th July, 1916	(k.)
Lieut. T. L. Purdon	18th June, 1916, to 19th July, 1916.	

Officer Commanding H.Q. Flight, 17th American Squadron :—

Lieut. H. McC. Bangs (U.S. A.S.) .... 11th Feb., 1918, to 17th April, 1918.

Armament Officer :—

Lieut. A. W. Sutton .... Jan., 1917, to April, 1917.

"A" FLIGHT.

FLIGHT COMMANDERS.

Captain E. H. Mitchell, M.C.	1st Oct., 1915, to 29th April, 1916.	(K.)
Captain J. O. Andrews, D.S.O., M.C.	30th April, 1916, to 5th Dec., 1916.	
Captain H. A. Wood	20th Dec., 1916, to 11th Mar., 1917.	
Captain P. F. J. Kent	11th Mar., 1197, to 12th July, 1917.	
Captain H. W. Woollett, D.S.O., M.C.	13th July, 1917, to 19th Aug., 1917.	
Captain B. P. G. Beanlands, M.C.	19th Aug., 1917, to 22nd Mar., 1918.	(W.) (k.)
Captain I. D. R. MacDonald, M.C., D.F.C.	22nd Mar., 1918, to 21st June, 1918.	
†Captain T. F. Hazell, D.S.O., M.C., D.F.C.	28th June, 1918, to 18th Oct., 1918.	
Captain D. Carruthers	18th Oct., 1918, to 16th Dec., 1918.	
Captain S. L. G. Pope	18th Dec., 1918, to 3rd Feb., 1919.	

FLYING OFFICERS.

*2nd-Lieut. J. O. Andrews, D.S.O., M.C.	25th Jan., 1916, to 30th April, 1916.	
Lieut. E. N. Clifton	Jan., 1916, to 29th Feb., 1916.	
†Lieut. S. E. Cowan, M.C.	1st Jan., 1916, to 1st Oct., 1916.	(k.)
2nd-Lieut. J. J. Breen	19th Mar., 1916, to 17th Dec., 1916.	
†Lieut. F. W. Honnet	17th May, 1916, to 6th August, 1916.	
2nd-Lieut. T. S. Sharpe	27th May, 1916, to 14th July, 1916.	
2nd-Lieut. K. P. McNamara	16th June, 1916, to 29 June, 1916.	(K.)
2nd-Lieut. S. E. Pither	22nd June, 1916, to 23 July, 1916.	
2nd-Lieut. A. E. McKay	Dec., 1916, to 14 Mar., 1917.	
2nd-Lieut. G. Wigglesworth	1st July, 1916, to 8th July, 1916.	(K.)
2nd-Lieut. A. E. Glew	12th July, 1916, to 8th Sept., 1916.	(K.)
†2nd-Lieut. R. H. M. S. Saundby, M.C.	25th July, 1916, to 14th Feb., 1917.	
2nd-Lieut. E. R. Yates	31st July, 1916, to 2nd Oct., 1916.	
2nd-Lieut. W. Roche Kelly	10th Aug., 1916, to 14th April, 1917.	
2nd-Lieut. R. S. Capon	16th Aug., 1916, to 31st Aug., 1916.	
2nd-Lieut. C. P. V. Roche	1st Sept., 1916, to 30th Sept., 1916.	(W.)
2nd-Lieut. J. H. Crutch	16th Sept., 1916, to 24th Jan., 1917.	
2nd-Lieut. F. B. Sedgwick	30th Sept., 1916, to 24th Mar., 1917.	
2nd-Lieut. N. Middlebrook	30th Sept., 1916, to 10th Oct., 1916.	(P.)
2nd-Lieut. W. C. Crawford	11th Oct., 1916, to 12th Dec., 1916.	(K.)
*2nd-Lieut. K. Crawford	17th Oct., 1916, to 21st Mar., 1917.	(k.)
*2nd-Lieut. H. W. Woollett, D.S.O., M.C.	30th Nov., 1916, to 13th July, 1917.	
2nd-Lieut. J. H. Histed	15th Dec., 1916, to 3rd Jan., 1917.	
Lieut. E. H. Tatton	18th Feb., 1917, to 24th June, 1917.	(k.)
2nd-Lieut. J. K. Ross	15th Mar., 1917, to 5th April, 1917.	(K.)
Lieut. J. G. Aronson	23rd Mar., 1917, to 18th May, 1917.	
2nd-Lieut. B. L. Blofield	23rd Mar., 1917, to 17th Sept., 1917.	
2nd-Lieut. E. Kent	6th April, 1917, to 8th April, 1917.	(K.)
Lieut. J. H. H. Goodall	19th May, 1917, to 24th May, 1917.	(P.)
2nd-Lieut. C. E. Woodhams	15th April, 1917, to 28th Aug., 1917.	
2nd-Lieut. R. C. Davies	24th May, 1917, to 2nd Nov., 1917.	(W.)
2nd-Lieut. D. Sutherland	24th June, 1917, to 27th Jan., 1918.	
2nd-Lieut. E. Churcher	4th July, 1917, to 7th July, 1917.	(k.)
2nd-Lieut. G. P. Robertson	5th Sept., 1917, to 10th Sept., 1917.	(P.)
Lieut. H. V. L. Tubbs	10th Sept., 1917, to 21st Mar., 1918.	(W.)
2nd-Lieut. R. J. Underhill	13th Sept., 1917, to 24th Sept., 1917.	
2nd-Lieut. R. G. Hammersley	25th Sept., 1917, to 1st Mar., 1918.	
2nd-Lieut. G. W. Forbes	10th Oct., 1917, to 18th Oct., 1917.	(K.)
Lieut. F. L. Watson	19th Oct., 1917, to 24th Oct., 1917.	
2nd-Lieut. A. P. C. Wigan	31st Oct., 1917, to 6th Mar., 1918.	(P.)
2nd-Lieut. I. D. Campbell	3rd Nov., 1917, to 30th Nov., 1917.	(K.)
2nd-Lieut. J. J. Dawe	20th Nov., 1917, to 7th June, 1918.	(K.)
2nd-Lieut. J. W. Bell	2nd Dec., 1917, to 3rd Dec., 1917.	
2nd-Lieut. D. M. Clementz	11th Dec., 1917, to 6th Mar., 1918.	(K.)
2nd-Lieut. H. D. Barton, D.F.C.	3rd Jan., 1918, to 6th Mar., 1918.	
2nd-Lieut. R. G. M. McRae	24th Jan., 1918, to 28th Jan., 1918.	(K.)
2nd-Lieut. E. A. Whitehead	24th Feb., 1918, to 13th Mar., 1918.	(K.)
2nd-Lieut. J. A. Miller	8th Mar., 1918, to 28th Mar., 1918.	(K.)
2nd-Lieut. G. B. Foster, D.F.C.	8th Mar., 1918, to 27th Aug., 1918.	
2nd-Lieut. H. B. Redler, M.C.	11th Mar., 1918, to 1st April, 1918.	(k.)
Lieut. F. V. Heakes	14th Mar., 1918, to 28th Mar., 1918.	(W.)

FLYING OFFICERS.—*Contd.*

Lieut. E. P. Crossen	26th Mar., 1918, to 8th Oct., 1918.	
2nd-Lieut. J. H. Southey	30th Mar., 1918, to 23rd Oct., 1918.	
Lieut. C. W. Davison	12th April, 1918, to 29th May, 1918.	(k.)
Lieut. H. F. Balmer	30th May, 1918, to 14th July, 1918.	
Lieut. J. R. Watkins	31st May, 1918, to 8th Aug., 1918.	(W.)
Lieut. W. C. Sterling	8th June, 1918, to 3rd Oct., 1918.	(K.)
Lieut. F. E. Beauchamp	10th July, 1918, to 8th Aug., 1918.	(P.)
2nd-Lieut. I. D. R. MacDonald, M.C., D.F.C.	11th July, 1917, to 15th Mar., 1918.	
2nd-Lieut. J. S. Haigh	9th Aug., 1918, to 15th Aug., 1918.	(K.)
2nd-Lieut. A. L. Bloom	9th Aug., 1918, to 30th Dec., 1918.	
2nd-Lieut. J. R. Woods	16th Aug., 1918, to 20th Dec., 1918.	
2nd-Lieut. H. J. C. Seymour	25th Aug., 1918, to 28th Jan., 1919.	
2nd-Lieut. P. W. Johnson	3rd Oct., 1918, to 3rd Feb., 1919.	
2nd-Lieut. L. G. Farrant	11th Oct., 1918, to 22nd Oct., 1918.	
2nd-Lieut. A. Wren	14th Oct., 1918, to 3rd Feb., 1919.	
Lieut. V. H. Simmers	23rd Oct., 1918, to 26th Jan., 1919.	
2nd-Lieut. N. G. Forester	13th Dec., 1918, to 3rd Feb., 1919.	

N.C.O. PILOT.

Sergeant W. Piercy	16th July, 1916, to 19th Aug., 1916.

"B" FLIGHT.

FLIGHT COMMANDERS.

Captain R. E. A. W. Hughes-Chamberlain	Dec., 1915, to 16th August, 1916.	(W.)
Captain D. M. Tidmarsh, M.C.	16th Aug., 1916, to 13th Oct., 1916.	
Captain P. A. Langan Byrne, D.S.O.	14h Oct., 1916, to 16th Oct., 1916.	(K.)
Captain H. W. Von Poelnitz	18th Oct., 1916, to 14th April, 1917.	(k.)
Captain W. T. Hall	14th April, 1917, to 19th May, 1917.	(K.)
Captain S. Dalrymple	22nd May, 1917, to 12th July, 1917.	
Captain H. E. Read	3rd Aug., 1917, to 10th Aug., 1917.	(K.)
Captain T. C. Arnot	22nd Aug., 1917, to 3rd Sept., 1917.	
Captain W. B. Ives	30th Sept., 1917, to 6th Dec., 1917.	
Captain A. J. Brown, M.C.	6th Dec., 1917, to 15th Mar., 1918.	
Captain A. K. Cowper, M.C.	24th Mar., 1918, to 11th April, 1918.	
Captain C. N. Lowe, M.C., D.F.C.	19th April, 1918, to 3rd Sept., 1918.	
Captain W. H. Longton, D.F.C., A.F.C.	27th Sept., 1918, to 29th Dec., 1918.	
Captain B. K. D. Robertson, A.F.C.	17th Jan., 1919, to 3rd Feb., 1919.	

FLYING OFFICERS.

*2nd-Lieut. D. M. Tidmarsh, M.C.	Jan., 1916, to 16th Aug., 1916.	
Lieut. R. H. B. Ker	Jan., 1916, to 19th July, 1916.	
2nd-Lieut. E. A. Cave	Jan., 1916, to 13th Feb., 1916.	(K.)
Lieut. N. P. Manfield	15th Feb., 1916, to 9th Sept., 1916.	(K.)
Lieut. C. M. B. Chapman, M.C.	23rd May, 1916, to 4th Aug., 1916.	(k.)
Lieut. D. H. Gray	30th May, 1916, to 3rd July, 1916.	(K.)
2nd-Lieut. A. E. McKay	30th June, 1916, to Dec., 1916.	
2nd-Lieut. H. C. Evans, D.S.O.	4th July, 1916, to 3rd Sept., 1916.	(K.)
Lieut. S. C. H. Begbie	31st July, 1916, to 23rd Mar., 1917.	(k.)
2nd-Lieut. J. N. Holtom	3rd Aug., 1916, to 11th Aug., 1916.	
2nd-Lieut. L. C. Burcher	10th Aug., 1916, to 14th Sept., 1916.	
*Lieut. P. A. Langan Byrne, D.S.O.	11th Aug., 1916, to 14th Oct., 1916.	(K.)
2nd-Lieut. W. E. Nixon	10th Sept., 1916, to 21st Oct., 1916.	
2nd-Lieut. D. E. Evans	15th Sept., 1916, to Dec., 1916.	
2nd-Lieut. E. Lewis	1st Oct., 1916, to 26th Dec., 1916.	(K.)
Lieut. C. Butler	17th Oct., 1916, to 17th May, 1917.	
Lieut. C. R. Keary	22nd Oct., 1916, to 26th June, 1917.	
2nd-Lieut. G. W. Shuter	8th Dec, 1916, to 4th Aug., 1917.	
*Captain H. E. Read	1st Jan., 1917, to 3rd Aug., 1917.	(K.)
*2nd-Lieut. T. C. Arnot	21st Jan., 1917, to 22nd Aug., 1917.	
*2nd-Lieut. W. T. Hall	30th Jan., 1917, to 14th April, 1917.	(K.)
2nd-Lieut. M. A. White	14th April, 1917, to 23rd April, 1917.	(K.)

2nd-Lieut. H. J. McCracken	25th April, 1917, to 18th May, 1917.	
2nd-Lieut. W. H. Statham	11th May, 1917, to 6th Nov., 1917.	
†2nd-Lieut. A. Hepburn	16th May, 1917, to 3rd Jan., 1918.	
2nd-Lieut. E. W. Everiss	22nd May, 1917, to 12th Nov., 1917.	
2nd-Lieut. E. G. Johnston	26th June, 1917, to 10th Jan., 1918.	
2nd-Lieut. J. G. White	11th July, 1917, to 26th Aug., 1917.	(K.)
Lieut. J. D. McCall	Aug., 1917.	(k.)
*2nd-Lieut. A. K. Cowper, M.C.	26th Aug., 1917, to 24th Mar., 1918.	
2nd-Lieut. R. S. J. Dynes	5th Sept., 1917, to 27th Jan., 1918.	
2nd-Lieut. A. Taylor	16th Sept. ,1917, to 26th Sept., 1917.	(P.)
2nd-Lieut. P. H. Burt	27th Sept., 1917, to 5th Oct., 1917.	
2nd-Lieut. H. B. Richardson, M.C.	14th Nov., 1917, to 29th April, 1918.	
2nd-Lieut. W. F. Poulter	5th Dec., 1917, to 5th Mar., 1918.	(K.)
2nd-Lieut. C. H. Sharp	16th Dec., 1917, to 1st Jan., 1918.	
Lieut. D. N. Ross, D.C.M., M.M.	2nd Feb., 1918, to 17th Feb., 1918.	(K.)
2nd-Lieut. R. T. Mark, M.C.	10th Jan., 1917, to 28th May, 1918.	
2nd-Lieut. E. W. Lindeburg	8th Feb., 1918, to 6th July, 1918.	
2nd-Lieut. P. J. Nolan, D.F.C.	20th Feb., 1918, to 9th April, 1918.	(W.K.)
2nd-Lieut. R. H. Kirkaldy	6th Mar., 1918, to 25th Mar., 1918.	(M.)
†2nd-Lieut. C. M. G. Farrell, D.F.C.	11th Mar., 1918, to 30th Aug., 1918.	
*2nd-Lieut. J. Palmer	26th Mar., 1918, to 11th Oct., 1918.	
2nd-Lieut. E. T. Hendrie	24th Mar., 1918, to 12th April, 1918.	(W.)
Lieut. E. Harrison	28th Mar., 1918, to 17th May, 1918.	(K.)
2nd-Lieut. H. B. Redler, M.C.	1st April, 1918, to 23rd April, 1918.	(k.)
Lieut. E. G. McMurtrie	9th April, 1918, to 28th May, 1918.	
Lieut. R. A. Slipper	14th April, 1918, to 4th May, 1918.	(W.P.)
Lieut. B. Stefanson	17th April, 1918, to 21st April, 1918.	
Lieut. H. J. Youngman	19th May, 1918, to 4th June, 1918.	
Lieut. F. S. Passmore	29th May, 1918, to 11th Aug., 1918.	
Lieut. W. J. Miller	5th June, 1918, to 17th Sept., 1918.	(M.)
Lieut. R. K. Rose	26th June, 1918, to 7th Oct., 1918.	
Lieut. G. E. Wales	7th July, 1918, to 25th Oct., 1918.	
Lieut. J. A. Rorison (U.S., A.S.)	14th Aug., 1918, to 12th Sept., 1918.	
Lieut. R. A. Pertus	22nd Aug., 1918, to 29th Aug., 1918.	(K.)
Lieut. E. P. Larrabee	28th Aug., 1918, to 20th Sept., 1918.	(W.P.)
2nd-Lieut. R. U. Fuller	31st Aug., 1918, to 3rd Feb., 1919.	
Lieut. E. Carpenter	14th Sept., 1918, to 3rd Oct., 1918	(M.)
2nd-Lieut. E. L. Allanson	19th Sept., 1918, to 13th Oct., 1918.	
Lieut. C. A. Bissonette	24th Sept., 1918, to 3rd Feb., 1919.	
2nd-Lieut. H. V. Evans	4th Oct., 1918, to 3rd Feb., 1919.	
2nd-Lieut. T. A. Lawrence	5th Oct., 1918, to 8th Oct., 1918.	
Lieut. A. A. Cresswell	5th Oct., 1918, to 26th Jan., 1919.	
2nd-Lieut. G. Abrahams	10th Oct., 1918, to 3rd Feb., 1919	
2nd-Lieut. J. V. Flanagan	19th Oct., 1918, to 3rd Feb., 1919	

N.C.O. PILOT.

Corporal W. Goy	18th July, to 10th Aug., 1916.

"C" FLIGHT.

FLIGHT COMMANDERS.

2nd-Lieut. E. A. C. Archer	Jan., 1916, to 9th Feb., 1916.	(K.)
Captain A. M. Wilkinson, D.S.O.	9th Feb., 1916, to 13th Oct., 1916.	
Captain S. H. Long, D.S.O., M.C.	13th Oct., 1916, to 17th Mar., 1917.	
Captain H. W. G. Jones	11th Mar., 1917, to 21st Mar., 1917.	
Captain K. Crawford	21st Mar., 1917, to 3rd July, 1917.	(k.)
Captain L. A. Hardwick-Terry	13th July, 1917, to 31st Aug., 1917.	(K.)
Captain L. V. Thorowgood	16th Sept., 1917, to 2nd Nov., 1917.	(W.)
Captain R. C. Davies	2nd Nov., 1917, to 25th Jan., 1918.	(W.)
Captain J. S. Ralston, M.C.	29th Jan., 1918, to 16th Feb., 1918.	(W.)
Captain G. E. H. McElroy, ~~D.S.O.~~, M.C, D.F.C.	19th Feb., 1918, to 10th April, 1918.	(k.)
Captain G. O. Johnson, M.C.	12th April, 1918, to 19th June, 1918.	
Captain W. Selwyn, D.F.C.	21st June, 1918, to 26th Aug., 1918.	
Captain H. D. Barton, D.F.C.	27th Aug., 1918, to 10th Oct., 1918	
Captain J. Palmer	11th Oct., 1918, to Cadre.	

FLYING OFFICERS.

2nd-Lieut. S. J. Sibley	Dec., 1915, to 3rd Sept., 1916.	(W.)
2nd-Lieut. A. M. Wilkinson, D.S.O.	16th Jan., 1916, to 9th Feb., 1916.	
2nd-Lieut. O. Lerwill	16th Jan., 1916, to 26th Mar., 1916.	(P.)
2nd-Lieut. W. A. C. Morgan, M.C.	10th Feb., 1916, to 16th Oct., 1916.	
2nd-Lieut. D. Wilson, M.C.	31st Mar., 1916, to 30th July, 1916.	(K.)
†2nd-Lieut. A. G. Knight, D.S.O., M.C.	30th May, 1916, to 16th May, 1916.	(k.)
2nd-Lieut. K. H. Riversdale-Elliott	9th June, 1916, to 5th July, 1916.	
*2nd-Lieut. H. A. Wood	16th June, 1916, to 20th Dec., 1916.	
2nd-Lieut. C. Kerr	9th July, 1916, to 8th Sept., 1916.	(P.)
Captain R. K. Thomson	31st July, 1916, to 27th Aug., 1916.	
2nd-Lieut. J. V. Bowring	2nd Sept., 1916, to 14th Sept., 1916.	(P.)
2nd-Lieut. L. A. Briggs	4th Sept., 1916, to 11th Sept., 1916.	(P.)
2nd-Lieut. E. C. Pashley	15th Sept., 1916, to 17th Mar., 1917.	(K.)
2nd-Lieut. R. G. Fordham	1st Oct., 1916, to 12th Nov., 1916.	
2nd-Lieut. H. B. Begg	22nd Oct., 1916, to 13th Nov., 1916.	(K.)
2nd-Lieut. S. Cockerell	11th Nov., 1916, to 17th June, 1917.	(W.)
2nd-Lieut. W. F. T. James	24th Nov., 1916, to 5th Jan., 1917.	(W.)
2nd-Lieut. D. E. Evans	Dec., 1916, to 20th May, 1917.	
*Lieut. L. A. Hardwick-Terry	19th Jan., 1917, to 13th July, 1917.	(K.)
*2nd-Lieut. A. J. Brown, M.C.	21st Mar., 1917, to 6th Dec., 1917.	
2nd-Lieut. H. C. Cutler	27th Mar., 1917, to 10th May, 1917.	(K.)
*2nd-Lieut. W. B. Ives	12th April, 1917, to 30th Sept., 1917.	
Lieut. J. H. Jephson	27th May, 1917, to 18th Dec., 1917.	
2nd-Lieut. N. H. Albury	22nd Aug., 1917, to 15th Sept., 1917.	(K.)
2nd-Lieut. A. W. Peacock	5th Sept., 1917, to 9th Sept., 1917.	(K.)
2nd-Lieut. G. H. Hunter	5th Sept., 1917, to 5th Feb., 1918.	
2nd-Lieut. P. A. McDougall, M.C.	15th Sept., 1917, to 12th Mar., 1918.	(W.)
2nd-Lieut. J. W. Jackson	5th Oct., 1917, to 22nd Jan., 1918.	
2nd-Lieut. C. H. Crosbee	16th Nov., 1917, to 26th Feb., 1918.	(W. & P.)
Lieut. M. L. Howard	24th Jan., 1918, to 22nd Feb., 1918.	
2nd-Lieut. E. F. Wright	24th Jan., 1918, to 15th Mar., 1918.	
Lieut. J. A. E. R. Daley, D.F.C.	14th Mar., 1918, to 8th July, 1918.	(K.)
2nd-Lieut. W. F. Warner	14th Mar., 1918, to 24th Mar., 1918.	(W.)
2nd-Lieut. T. T. B. Hellett	3rd Mar., 1918, to 22nd Sept., 1918.	
2nd-Lieut. E. B. Wilson	19th Mar., 1918, to 25th June, 1918.	(W.)
2nd-Lieut. W. C. Lambert, D.F.C.	24th Mar., 1918, to 21st Aug., 1918.	
2nd-Lieut. A. Wren	20th June, 1918, to 14th Oct., 1918.	
2nd-Lieut. T. M. Harries, D.F.C.	24th June, 1918, to 25th Jan., 1919.	
Lieut. H. L. Bair, D.F.C. (U.S. A.S.)	5th July, 1918, to 19th Sept., 1918.	
Lieut. W. G. C. Geraghty	18th Aug., 1918, to 3rd Feb., 1919.	
Lieut. J. T. Menzies	22nd Aug., 1918, to 31st Oct., 1918.	
Lieut. N. H. Barlow	3rd Sept., 1918, to 1st Jan., 1919.	
2nd-Lieut W. B. Thomson	25th Sept., 1918, to 3rd Feb., 1919.	
2nd-Lieut. R. A. Eldridge	7th Oct., 1918, to 18th Jan., 1919.	
2nd-Lieut. G. H. Whitehead	1st Nov., 1918, to 3rd Feb., 1919.	

N.C.O. PILOT.

*Sergeant S. Cockerell	1st Sept., 1916, to 10th Oct., 1916.	(W.)

Abbreviations :—
K. Killed whilst serving in No. 24 Squadron.
k. Killed since leaving No. 24 Squadron.
W. Wounded.
P. Prisoner.
M. Missing.
* Promoted in Squadron.
† Promoted on leaving Squadron.

ROLL OF WARRANT OFFICERS, NON-COMMISSIONED OFFICERS AND MEN.

1.—SERGEANT-MAJORS.

Name.	Regimental No.	From	Promotion and Service. (In No. 24 Squadron.) Joined.	Left.
Gardiner, J. R., M.S.M.	178	—	In England.	20th Jan., 1918
Blanchard, F. C.	5892	2 a.m.	In England when Squadron was being formed.	16th Aug., 1917
Moores, W. R.	14140	2 a.m.		22nd June, 1917
Hummerstone, G.	4098	1 a.m.		19th May, 1917
Winch, D. F.	11630	2 a.m.		4th Mar., 1917
Treavis, W. A. H.	S.R.5			3rd Nov., 1916
Little, L.	34	—		13th July, 1916
Tanner, R.	700	—	5th Dec., 1916	24th Feb., 1918
Burford, E.	2253	—	14th Jan., 1918	27th Mar., 1918
Schofield, F., M.S.M.	5974	—	1st Mar., 1918	1st Jan., 1919
King, L. C.	21306	—	1st June, 1918	Cadre

2.—FLIGHT-SERGEANTS.

Name.	Regimental No.	From	Joined.	Left.
Fisher, A. J., M.S.M.	10589	2 a.m.		Cadre.
Edwards, H.	3452	2 a.m.	In England when Squadron was being formed.	2nd Feb., 1919
Thould, F. T.	11197	2 a.m.		28th Jan., 1919
Ord, F.	14111	2 a.m.		20th Oct., 1918
Hipwell, J. T.	11189	2 a.m.		11th Oct., 1918
Linter, H. G.	5591	2 a.m.		20th May, 1918
†Heales, H.	6859	1 a.m.		19th Dec., 1917
Ward, S. E.	10958	2 a.m.		19th Nov., 1917
Wormald, E.	1808	—		1st Aug., 1917
Workman, C. H.	15964	2 a.m.		1st Aug., 1917
Bond, C.	388	—		18th Nov., 1916
Greenhalgh, F.	2087	—		15th Oct., 1916
Clarkson, C. H.	5832	—		19th Aug., 1916
Allen, C. F.	99	—		11th June, 1916
Cummins, T. W.	632	—		7th May, 1916
Tealby, F. R. V.	3430	Corpl.	10th May, 1916	Cadre.
Langston, J. H.	24317	2 a.m.	27th May, 1916	1st Feb., 1919

3.—SERGEANTS.

Name.	Regimental No.	From	Joined.	Left.
Percy, R. A. E.	5514	2 a.m.	In England when Squadron was being formed.	2nd Feb., 1919
Cox, L. C.	5964	2 a.m.		2nd Feb., 1919
Brown, H.	6131	2 a.m.		2nd Feb., 1919
Haines, G.	6200	2 a.m.		2nd Feb., 1919
Peters, C. H.	9227	2 a.m.		2nd Feb., 1919
Hoskins, V. E. T.	11162	2 a.m.		2nd Feb., 1919
Welch, J. W.	15266	2 a.m.		2nd Feb., 1919
Tingle, A. W.	3570	2 a.m.		28th Nov., 1918
Richardson, L. A.	5722	2 a.m.		27th Oct., 1918
Amos, A.	4007	2 a.m.		20th Aug., 1918
Evans, W. L.	12226	2 a.m.		29th April, 1918
Duns, R. A.	10793	2 a.m.		12th April, 1918
Bulstrode, S.	6402	2 a.m.		18th Mar., 1918
Winn, D.	5979	2 a.m.		12th Feb., 1918
Hurst, C. G.	15631	2 a.m.		18th Feb., 1918
Pringle, H. G.	9229	1 a.m.		30th Oct., 1917
Soothill, F.	3623	Sergt.		19th July, 1917

3.—SERGEANTS.—*Contd.*

Name.	Regimental No.	From	Promotion and Service. (In No. 24 Squadron.) Joined.	Left.
Perry, J.	11168	2 a.m.	In England when Squadron was being formed.	19th May, 1917
Exton, H. G.	5667	—		19th Feb., 1917
Patrick, H.	5914	—		19th Jan., 1917
Harvey, C. R.	2223	1 a.m.		18th Dec., 1916
Coxall, A. C.	3643	—		31st Oct., 1916
Ridley, P.	10795	2 a.m.		17th Sept., 1916
Burtenshaw, W.	239	—		27th Aug., 1916
Lacey, G.	4577	—		17th Aug., 1916
Dobson, E. H.	934	—		28th Mar., 1916
Wilson, A.	14476	2 a.m.	20th April, 1916	2nd Feb., 1919
French, W. L.	16823	2 a.m.	20th April, 1916	28th Jan., 1919
Sterling, J. W.	24345	2 a.m.	27th May, 1916	3rd Feb., 1919
Garland, L.	18973	2 a.m.	1st July, 1916	Cadre.
Wilson, A.	29518	2 a.m.	8th July, 1916	2nd Feb., 1919
Goy, W. S.	2196	Corpl.	18th July, 1916	19th April, 1917
Tait, J.	5896	1 a.m.	20th July, 1916	19th Mar., 1917
Whitworth, J.	30273	2 a.m.	31st July, 1916	5th Jan., 1919
Green, W.	11110	Corpl.	5th Dec., 1916	Cadre.
Taylor, E.	882	—	11th Dec, 1916	14th Feb., 1916
Dearman, E.	14014	2 a.m.	23rd Dec., 1916	28th Dec., 1918
Brooks, W.	14137	1 a.m.	31st Jan., 1917	20th Sept., 1918
Vincent, W. B. H.	2820	—	9th Feb., 1918	4th May, 1918

4.—CORPORALS.

Name.	Regimental No.	From	Joined.	Left.
Calloway, J.	5983	2 a.m.	In England when Squadron was being formed.	3rd Feb., 1919
Cox, F. S.	6201	2 a.m.		3rd Feb., 1919
Addison, S. F.	11146	2 a.m.		3rd Feb., 1919
Morey, B.	10831	2 a.m.		1st Feb., 1919
Jefferson, B.	8500	2 a.m.		25th Jan., 1919
Cox, J. L.	10858	2 a.m.		25th Jan., 1919
Wheeler, L. E.	6441	2 a.m.		17th Nov., 1918
Chorley, E. T.	5860	2 a.m.		15th Oct., 1918
Gazard, F. H.	10793	2 a.m.		7th Sept., 1918
Blower, G. W.	15708	2 a.m.		28th Nov., 1917
Lampard, T. S.	10829	—		16th Sept., 1917
Cook, E.	6114	2 a.m.		13th Sept., 1917
Broad, E. M.	2311	1 a.m.		19th Aug., 1917
Pringle, H.	3938	2 a.m.		26th April, 1917
Summers, P. J.	10738	—		26th Mar., 1917
Hawkesford, R.	10741	—		26th Feb., 1917
Robbins, L. C.	6234	—		26th Jan., 1917
Jenkins, J. L.	2134	—		26th Dec., 1916
Pullar, S. D. W.	15966	—		28th Nov., 1916
Greenaway, W.	5982	—		25th Nov., 1916
Winter, A.	11016	—		22nd Oct., 1916
Warren, J. A.	10845	—		20th Aug., 1916
Sanderson, A.	10876	—		2nd July, 1916
Eley, J. S.	849	—		18th June, 1916
Westwood, A.	3646	—		14th May, 1916
Latham, G. A.	3029	1 a.m.	1st Mar., 1916	24th Sept., 1916
Cocks, A. F.	6594	2 a.m.	10th May, 1916	20th July, 1918
Parry, H. L.	24392	2 a.m.	27th May, 1916	20th Oct., 1918
Spencer, P. D.	24335	2 a.m.	27th May, 1916	17th June, 1917
Matthews, H.	1268	—	27th May, 1916	10th Sept., 1916
Daws, G.	29328	2 a.m.	3rd Aug., 1916	Cadre.
Bradbury, L.	42051	2 a.m.	14th Sept, 1916	25th Jan., 1919
Tilley, E.	2278	1 a.m.	14th Sept, 1916	26th Oct., 1918
Gradwell, V.	13933	1 a.m.	13th Nov., 1916	3rd Feb., 1919
McKenzie, R.	40277	2 a.m.	16th Feb., 1917	3rd Feb., 1919
Eatock, H.	46733	2 a.m.	19th May, 1917	27th Jan., 1919
Harman, C. B.	31960	—	31st Jan., 1918	3rd Feb., 1919
Hinton, F. M.	39871	—	22nd Feb., 1918	20th June, 1918

5.—AIR MECHANICS (1st Class).

Name.	Regimental No.	From	Promotion and Service. (In No. 24 Squadron.) Joined.	Left.
Evens, E.	1924	2 a.m.	In England when Squadron was being formed.	4th Feb., 1919
Wood, B. L.	10960	2 a.m.		3rd Feb., 1919
Searle, R. V.	15965	2 a.m.		Cadre.
Smith, W. E.	10837	2 a.m.		28th Jan., 1919
Mundy, A. J.	11183	2 a.m.	In England when Squadron was being formed.	26th Jan., 1919
Webb, L.	14697	2 a.m.		25th Jan., 1919
Allen, W. A. S.	15853	—		15th Jan., 1919
Nicholls, H. E.	11150	2 a.m.		5th Oct., 1918
Jones, W.	10693	—		20th Mar., 1918
Lee, F. R. V.	11214	—		26th Jan., 1918
Cotterell, C.	7676	—		26th Dec., 1917
Woolley, F.	5345	—		29th Nov., 1917
Oxford, S.	15972	2 a.m.		26th Nov., 1917
Meale, G. H.	11071	—		27th Oct., 1917
Harper, A.	6295	2 a.m.		20th Sept., 1917
Slinger, S.	4119	—		17th June, 1917
Wilkinson, A. J.	10847	2 a.m.		12th June, 1917
Ogden, J.	14062	—		8th April, 1917
Craghill, J. H.	6377	—		22nd Feb., 1917
Slum, A.	11229	—		30th Jan., 1917
Davies, G.	5016	—		26th Jan., 1917
Dally, R. H.	3684	—		8th Jan., 1917
Morley, C.	3626	—		7th Jan., 1917
Hawes, H.	4252	—		26th Dec., 1916
Webb, A. V.	10846	2 a.m.		22nd Dec., 1916
Neal, E.	9292	—		2nd Dec., 1916
Sleet, W. J.	5455	—		28th Nov., 1916
Wood, S. J.	11185	—		25th Nov., 1916
Wilson, R.	11093	—		5th Nov., 1916
Stow, S. L.	11221	—		22nd Oct., 1916
Townend, E.	10748	—		24th Sept., 1916
Hodge, H.	7406	—		31st Aug., 1916
Scott, R. L.	15772	2 a.m.		28th Aug., 1916
Woods, L.	4373	—		27th Aug., 1916
Eaton, J. F.	5346	—		24th Aug., 1916
Pritchard, W. P.	3790	—		16th July, 1916
Holden, W.	10886	—		18th June, 1916
Court, N.	11021	—		12th June, 1916
Brown, C.	6053	—		21st May, 1916
Lewis, F.	8070	—		14th May, 1916
Payne, R.	15820	2 a.m.	1st April, 1916	29th Jan., 1919
Rose, W.	22881	2 a.m.	1st April, 1916	16th Sept., 1917
Thompson, J.	25235	2 a.m.	12th April, 1916	Cadre.
Goldstein, J.	13238	2 a.m.	20th April, 1916	9th Mar., 1918
Clarke, A. G.	7097	—	10th May, 1916	21st Aug., 1918
Cunliffe, L. H.	3733	2 a.m.	10th May, 1916	9th Sept., 1917
Wallman, A.	8740	—	27th May, 1916	21st Aug., 1916
Swaine, J. R.	9969	—	27th May, 1916	21st Aug., 1916
Grinton, T.	24374	2 a.m.	27th May, 1916	Cadre.
Macklin, T. H.	23274	2 a.m.	27th May, 1916	16th Nov., 1918
Mathews, G. H.	19515	2 a.m.	27th May, 1916	1st Nov., 1918
Peat, D. P.	24376	2 a.m.	27th May, 1916	15th May, 1918
Sim, A.	24375	2 a.m.	27th May, 1916	26th July, 1917
Miller, J. A.	23124	2 a.m.	27th May, 1916	29th Jan., 1917
Stevenson, E. W.	25288	2 a.m.	9th June, 1916	24th June, 1917
Smith, E.	18798	2 a.m.	9th June, 1916	21st Mar., 1917
Woolfenden, E. T.	18919	2 a.m.	27th June, 1916	28th Jan., 1919
Hampson, J.	25990	2 a.m.	8th July, 1916	25th Jan., 1919
Howard, H.	33395	2 a.m.	25th July, 1916	27th Aug., 1917
Crofts, S.	29334	2 a.m.	3rd Aug., 1916	27th May, 1918
Detheridge, A. J.	25489	2 a.m.	3rd Aug., 1916	15th May, 1918
Kirby, C. A.	36421	2 a.m.	3rd Aug., 1916	17th Aug., 1917
Weir, A. H.	26827	2 a.m.	3rd Aug., 1916	15th Mar., 1917
Ellis, F. T.	32629	2 a.m.	21st Aug., 1916	26th Jan., 1919
Ashby, R. A.	32627	2 a.m.	21st Aug., 1916	27th Sept., 1918
Wainer, B.	32628	2 a.m.	21st Aug., 1916	15th Dec., 1916

5.—AIR MECHANICS (1st Class).—*Contd.*

Name.	Regimental No.	From	Promotion and Service. (In No. 24 Squadron.) Joined.	Left.
Simpson, T.	32610	2 a.m.	25th Aug., 1916	1st Feb., 1919
Cooper, C. B.	28709	2 a.m.	29th Aug., 1916	29th Nov., 1917
Hartnell, A. G.	24116	2 a.m.	31st Aug., 1916	18th Nov., 1917
Green, A. G.	26720	2 a.m.	31st Aug., 1916	17th Aug., 1917
Orr, J.	15755	—	11th Sept., 1916	11th Feb., 1917
Pipe, A. H. A.	32106	2 a.m.	12th Sept., 1916	3rd Feb., 1919
Meek, H. M.	45294	2 a.m.	25th Sept., 1916	26th Mar., 1917
Thomas, A.	21202	2 a.m.	21st Oct., 1916	1st Feb., 1919
Turner, A. H. J.	10614	2 a.m.	21st Oct., 1916	6th May, 1918
Ayling F. H.	29345	2 a.m.	13th Nov., 1916	11th July, 1918
Gillies, P.	27228	2 a.m.	13th Nov., 1916	24th May, 1917
North, G.	38718	2 a.m.	16th Nov., 1916	27th June, 1918
Locke, H.	39091	2 a.m.	16th Nov., 1916	25th Feb., 1918
†Parry, J.	23867	2 a.m.	25th Nov., 1916	4th Feb, 1919
Morris, A.	17499	2 a.m.	8th Dec., 1916	Cadre.
Howard, C. W. J.	41001	2 a.m.	5th Jan., 1917	29th Oct., 1917
Cooper, A.	42739	2 a.m.	15th Jan., 1917	30th Jan., 1919
Shaw, C.	42538	2 a.m.	24th Jan., 1917	27th April, 1918
Jamie, E.	6573	2 a.m.	3rd Mar., 1917	1st Feb. 1919
Hardistie, S.	30809	—	11th Mar., 1917	3rd Feb., 1919
Cox, E. J.	39228	2 a.m.	11th Mar., 1917	27th Jan., 1919
Jones, G. W.	45413	2 a.m.	13th April, 1917	27th Jan., 1919
Gascoyne, P.	38689	2 a.m.	13th April, 1917	25th Jan., 1919
Gledhill, S.	55421	2 a.m.	2nd May, 1917	2nd Dec., 1918
Smith, J. W.	58415	2 a.m.	5th May, 1917	26th Aug., 1918
Clark, C. O. R.	37483	—	5th May, 1917	8th June, 1917
Riley, P.	20428	2 a.m.	26th May, 1917	27th July, 1918
Marshall, E.	20076	—	3rd June, 1917	22nd Oct., 1917
Ellis, J. C.	47685	2 a.m.	12th June, 1917	10th Jan., 1919
Williams, V.	6693	—	16th June, 1917	5th Sept., 1917
Elliott, J. W.	28734	2 a.m.	11th July, 1917	24th Sept., 1918
Roxburgh, J. S.	86816	2 a.m.	3rd Aug., 1917	3rd Feb., 1919
Lacey, J.	21077	—	4th Sept., 1917	16th Sept., 1917
Da Costa, S.	22742	—	16th Feb., 1918	Cadre.
Pollock, D. N.	23310	—	20th Mar., 1918	27th Aug., 1918
Cheshire, C.	17581	—	7th June, 1918	16th Aug., 1918
Harland, S. F.	25463	—	10th June, 1918	3rd Feb., 1919
Bowler, H. C.	13895	—	8th July, 1918	3rd Feb., 1919
Latham, N.	13479	—	4th Aug., 1918	8th Nov., 1918
Bishop, C.	6334	—	3rd Nov., 1918	3rd Feb., 1919
Wallace, W.	7241	—	3rd Nov., 1918	28th Jan., 1919
Hurrell, F. S.	29291	1 a.m.		Jan., 1919

6.—AIR MECHANICS (2nd Class).

Name.	Regimental No.	From	Joined.	Left.
Payne, E.	17277	—	In England when Squadron was being formed.	7th Sept., 1917
Underwood, J.	5496	—		26th July, 1917
Miller, J.	14210	—		24th June, 1917
Burrell, T. A.	10790	—		21st May, 1917
Luscombe, J.	12300	—		17th Feb., 1917
Martin, J.	3237	—		15th Feb., 1917
Earney, H. A.	15720	—		4th Feb., 1917
Jarvis, S. C.	16330	—		28th Jan., 1917
Sargeant, G. H.	15825	—		21st Jan., 1917
Myram, J.	6103	—		14th Jan., 1917
Brand, O. W. S.	11709	—		14th Jan., 1917
Myhill, S. C.	11018	—		8th Jan., 1917
Worn, F.	11095	—		6th Oct., 1916
Eccles, S. A.	12580	—		29th April, 1916
Ripon, H.	15616	—		31st Mar., 1916
Hall, J.	14702	—		10th Mar., 1916
Dent, F. W.	15482	—		5th Feb., 1916
Eversfield, J.	10965	2 a.m.		14th Feb., 1917
Browning, L. W.	4011	—	18th Feb., 1916	7th Jan., 1916
Birch, H.	6102	—	20th Feb., 1916	20th Aug., 1916
Simpson, J.	14216	—	12th April, 1916	13th April, 1916
Walton, F.	20873	—	27th May, 1916	17th Oct., 1917

6.—AIR MECHANICS (2ND CLASS).—*Contd.*

Name.	Regimental No.	From	Promotion and Service. (In No. 24 Squadron.) Joined.	Left.
Murdock, J.	24316	—	27th May, 1916	3rd Feb., 1917
Newstead, J. E.	23039	—	27th May, 1916	27th Nov., 1916
Gilbert, H.	24262	—	27th May, 1916	29th May, 1916
Ward, C. F.	13678	—	30th May, 1916	26th April, 1917
Goodwill, F.	17278	—	9th June, 1916	Cadre.
Randall, T.	27243	—	9th June, 1916	16th Oct., 1916
George, W. A.	22157	—	5th July, 1916	21st May, 1917
Wright, L.	29553	—	13th July, 1916	26th Jan., 1918
Simmons, C. G.	33387	—	25th July, 1916	21st Mar., 1917
Hartley, B.	33728	—	25th July, 1916	19th Dec., 1916
Elgy, V. C. H.	29359	2 a.m.	2nd Aug., 1916	11th Jan., 1917
Thomas, J. H.	16076	—	3rd Aug., 1916	16th Sept., 1917
Lymer, C. E.	36402	—	3rd Aug., 1916	26th June, 1917
Thewlis, J.	33819	—	25th Aug., 1916	28th Aug., 1916
Tice, W.	28449	—	11th Sept., 1916	21st May, 1917
Brown, L. C.	28447	—	11th Sept., 1916	8th Jan., 1917
Morgan, T. J.	21209	—	1st Oct., 1916	30th May, 1917
Brown, S. F. O.	21181	—	21st Oct., 1916	12th May, 1917
Racine, O. J.	37968	—	21st Oct., 1916	2nd Mar., 1917
Jenkinson, P.	41401	—	21st Oct., 1916	11th Feb., 1917
Day, E. C.	20138	2 a.m.	Nov., 1916	11th Dec., 1916
Lovell, G. H.	37752	—	5th Dec., 1916	25th Jan., 1919
Isted, C. H.	45891	—	5th Jan., 1917	30th Jan., 1917
Jewell, W. C.	24339	—	5th Jan., 1917	14th Jan., 1917
Holland, H.	40668	—	5th Jan., 1917	6th Jan., 1917
Valentine, J. H.	13925	—	9th Jan., 1917	12th Dec., 1917
Musson, W.	42675	—	9th Jan., 1917	11th June, 1917
Yarwood, A.	41688	—	10th Jan., 1917	26th Jan., 1919
Hallam, F.	51270	3 a.m.	10th Jan., 1917	25th Jan., 1919
Dow, W.	39466	—	10th Jan., 1917	30th April, 1917
Pugh, A.	52403	—	14th Jan., 1917	18th Jan., 1919
‡Poulter, F.	51345	—	9th Feb., 1917	3rd June, 1917
Reid, G. M.	4905	—	16th Feb., 1917	25th Jan., 1919
Frost, G. Y.	61652	—	20th Feb., 1917	8th Nov., 1917
Humphries, E. L.	58244	2 a.m.	Feb., 1917	16th Sept., 1917
Dodgson, F. S.	58939	2 a.m.	Feb., 1917	14th May, 1917
Dobson, T. S.	5893	—	3rd Mar., 1917	14th May, 1917
Gibson, W.	5662	—	3rd Mar., 1917	30th Mar., 1917
Spenser, T.	55262	3 a.m.	11th Mar., 1917	18th Jan., 1919
Martin, W.	24163	—	13th Mar., 1917	17th Nov., 1917
Cockerton, E. T.	60406	3 a.m.	13th Mar., 1917	29th Oct., 1917
Maybourne, T. G.	60300	—	13th Mar., 1917	17th June, 1917
Howe, A.	41021	—	13th Mar., 1917	15th Mar., 1917
Cundy, E. F.	39317	—	18th Mar., 1917	30th May, 1917
Dyer, W. H.	56712	—	23rd Mar., 1917	3rd Feb., 1919
Duce, G.	42283	—	1st April, 1917	27th Nov., 1917
Fleming, G. H.	52485	—	13th April, 1917	3rd Feb., 1919
Rimmer, G. B.	42347	—	13th April, 1917	27th Jan., 1919
Scott, A.	45384	—	13th April, 1917	22nd Oct., 1917
Alsom, L.	45389	—	13th April, 1917	7th Sept., 1917
Sharp, I.	54618	—	18th April, 1917	16th Sept., 1917
Poppleton, S.	53081	—	30th April, 1917	3rd Feb., 1919
Welch, W. C.	45811	—	30th April, 1917	10th Oct., 1918
Lees, E.	50655	—	30th April, 1917	4th Sept., 1917
Fitzmaurice, M.	53800	—	2nd May, 1917	3rd Feb., 1919
Bentley, F.	58626	—	5th May, 1917	9th July, 1918
Atkin, W.	64988	—	12th May, 1917	3rd Feb., 1919
Hammond, J. G.	67179	—	19th May, 1917	16th Sept., 1917
King, E. J. A.	67552	—	30th May, 1917	14th Oct., 1917
King, D. W.	67715	—	30th May, 1917	12th June, 1917
Dutnall, H.	64851	3 a.m.	31st May, 1917	6th May, 1918
Wright, S. R.	44703	—	3rd June, 1917	29th Jan., 1919
Ibbetson, W. T.	54525	—	7th June, 1917	16th Sept., 1917
Spiller, W. J.	42802	—	12th June, 1917	25th Feb., 1918
Potts, J. H.	47159	—	16th June, 1917	2nd Aug., 1917
Russell, W. G.	7514	—	17th June, 1917	26th Aug., 1917
Walton, H.	46204	—	22nd June, 1917	29th Jan., 1918

6.—AIR MECHANICS (2ND CLASS).—*Contd.*

Name.	Regimental No.		Promotion and Service. (In No. 24 Squadron.) From	Joined.		Left.
Noble, S. R.	54967	...	—	22nd June, 1917	...	25th June, 1917
Cockrell, W. F.	2191	...	—	7th July, 1917	...	16th Sept., 1917
Slater, G.	43119	...	—	29th July, 1917	...	16th May, 1918
Leng, W. F.	88003	...	—	8th Aug., 1917	...	21st Aug., 1918
Quinsey, W. J.	24446	...	—	31st Aug., 1917	...	18th Oct., 1917
Thomas, S. C.	21985	...	—	1st Sept., 1917	...	1st Feb.., 1919
Webster, S.	43893	...	—	4th Sept., 1917	...	18th Oct., 1917
Johnson, W. J.	77760	...	2 a.m.		...	16th Sept., 1917
Elsom, L.	45389	...	2 a.m.		...	7th Sept., 1917
Hulme, A.	69308	...	3 a.m.	29th Oct., 1917	...	13th Oct., 1918
Flook, F.	97283	...	2 a.m.	7th Nov., 1917	...	27th Dec., 1917
Dunbar, W.	103177	...	—	7th Nov., 1917	...	29th Nov., 1917
Morris, J. W.	14492	...	—	17th Nov., 1917	...	4th Feb., 1919
Oades, A.	87381	...	—	26th Nov., 1917	...	23rd Sept., 1918
Turner, A.	62810	...	—	1st Dec., 1917	...	3rd Feb., 1919
Henderson, C.	62298	...	—	1st Dec., 1917	...	25th Jan., 1918
Parsons, G. A.	5123	...	—	13th Dec., 1917	...	26th May, 1918
Scott, A.	87843	...	—	22nd Jan., 1918	...	3rd Feb., 1919
Fleet, B. S.	190154	...	2 a.m.	Jan., 1918	...	2nd Mar., 1918
Humphries, E. J.	41365	..	—	10th Feb., 1918	...	1st Feb., 1919
Robinson, A. R.	P.15416	...	—	10th Feb., 1918	...	28th Dec., 1918
Jelly, H. N.	P.24050	...	3 a.m.	12th Feb., 1918	...	28th Oct., 1918
Thornburgh, W.	36472	...	—	20th Feb., 1918	...	3rd Feb., 1919
Transley, F.	121941	...	—	20th Mar., 1918	...	15th May, 1918
Pauling, A.	94351	...	—	30th Mar., 1918	...	4th July, 1918
Holloway, F. P.	104176	...	—	31st Mar., 1918	...	1st April, 1918
Shaw, T. A.	P.41511	...	—	1st April, 1918	...	3rd Feb., 1919
Smith, D. W.	91516	...	—	1st April, 1918	...	25th Jan., 1919
Dainty, W. J.	103978	...	—	1st April, 1918	...	25th Jan., 1919
Gibson, E. J.	33513	...	—	6th May, 1918	...	26th May, 1918
Dearden, J. H.	69327	...	—	7th May, 1918	...	13th Jan., 1919
Park, W. H.	408448	...	—	12th May. 1918	...	15th May, 1918
Hickey, A.	7733	...	—	7th June, 1918	...	16th Aug., 1918
Young, H. W.	54048	...	—	7th June, 1918	...	25th July, 1918
Reeves, A.	104911	...	—	10th June, 1918	...	25th Jan., 1919
Sharp, E.	86249	...	—	14th July, 1918	...	3rd Feb., 1919
Need, J. S.	62141	...	3 a.m.	16th July, 1918	...	1st Feb., 1919
Nathan, A. A.	85058	...	3 a.m.	16th July, 1918	...	5th Nov., 1918
Martin, E.	78255	...	—	17th July, 1918	...	25th Jan, 1919
Staunton, E.	48051	...	—	17th July, 1918	...	24th Aug., 1918
Corcoran, J. W.	43297	...	—	18th Aug., 1918	...	3rd Feb., 1919
Cannell, W.	121986	...	3 a.m.	26th Aug., 1918	...	26th Jan., 1919
Smith, J.	L.8504	...	—	30th Jan., 1919	...	3rd Feb., 1919
Lock, N.	212022	...	—	30th Jan., 1919	...	3rd Feb., 1919

7.—AIR MECHANICS (3RD CLASS).

Name.	Regimental No.		From	Joined.		Left.
Worth, R.	29537	...	—	5th Dec., 1916	...	3rd Feb., 1919
Smith, N. J.	48677	...	—	5th Dec., 1916	...	3rd Feb., 1919
Carruthers, J. R.	75059	...	—	24th Dec., 1916	...	1st Feb., 1919
Hobson, H. E.	14975	...	—	21st Jan., 1917	...	17th Mar., 1918
Oddy, H.	127565	...	—	21st Jan., 1917	...	17th Mar., 1918
Meall, T. F.	61550	...	—	4th Feb., 1917	...	9th Jan., 1918
Lewis, T. F.	G.P.5203	...	—	4th Feb., 1917	...	7th Mar., 1917
Mills, G.	51518	...	—	4th Feb., 1917	...	12th Feb., 1917
Lusty, W. D.	45173	...	—	15th Feb., 1917	...	3rd Feb., 1919
Oliver, A. R.	45995	...	—	15th Feb., 1917	...	31st Oct., 1917
Ponsford, F. W.	46644	...	—	15th Feb., 1917	...	16th Sept., 1917
Ward, H.	51517	...	—	23rd Feb., 1917	...	3rd April, 1917
Porter, G.	16229	...	—	3rd Mar., 1917	...	7th Mar., 1917
Levy, J.	55834	...	—	13th Mar., 1917	...	2nd April, 1918
Vinycomb, J. K.	79712	...	—	7th June, 1917	...	13th June, 1917
Thomas, C.	51671	...	—	18th June, 1917	...	18th Oct., 1917
Ryan, W. H.	80051	...	—	22nd June, 1917	...	31st Oct., 1917
Rowles, G. A.	85492	...	—	9th Aug., 1917	...	21st Sept., 1917
Biningsley, T.	96055	...	—	7th Nov., 1917	...	15th Dec., 1917
Critchley, E.	63695	...	—	6th Dec., 1917	...	3rd Feb., 1919
Fisher, F.	97162	...	—	13th Dec., 1917	..	14th Dec., 1917
Gladstone, R.	98657	...	—	8th Jan., 1918	...	29th Jan., 1919

7.—AIR MECHANICS (3RD CLASS).—*Contd.*

Name.	Regimental No.	From	Promotion and Service. (In No. 24 Squadron.) Joined.	Left.
Flatley, W.	98656	—	8th Jan., 1918	13th Oct., 1918
Flint, B. S.	109154	—	10th Jan., 1918	2nd Feb., 1918
Cronan, J.	118866	—	11th Jan., 1918	8th Mar., 1918
Crewdson, A.	100857	—	8th Jan., 1918	3rd Feb., 1919
Moss, H.	108049	—	13th Jan., 1918	13th Jan., 1918
Topley, C. L.	62960	—	20th Jan., 1918	3rd. Feb., 1919
Slater, W.	127870	—	13th Feb., 1918	17th Mar., 1918
Wilson, H.	85854	—	22nd Feb., 1918	25th Jan., 1919
‡Priest, C. G. P.	121307	—	7th Mar., 1918	3rd Feb., 1919
Dennis, P. E.	94509	—	15th Mar., 1918	17th Jan., 1919
Nixon, G. T.	P.40650	—	13th Mar., 1918	5th Nov., 1918
Morrison, J. E.	P.79497	—	13th Mar., 1918	20th Mar., 1918
Lee, R. J.	104745	—	17th Mar., 1918	20th Mar., 1918
Dennis, J.	50595	—	31st Mar., 1918	25th Jan., 1919
Groome, J.	91371	—	31st Mar., 1918	23rd Sept., 1918
Arrowsmith, C. F.	120763	—	31st Mar., 1918	25th June, 1918
Stephens, A. G.	P.5694	—	1st April, 1918	3rd Feb., 1919
Grieve, W.	101855	—	9th June, 1918	7th Dec., 1918
Stead, C.	121027	—	9th June, 1918	16th Aug., 1918
Ingram, H.	408467	—	9th June, 1918	2nd Aug., 1918
Skinner, F.	87201	—	27th June, 1918	3rd Feb., 1919
Mason, H. H.	102514	—	26th July, 1918	Cadre.
Wallace, J.	266345	—	5th Aug., 1918	18th Aug., 1918
Cox, E.	61835	—	8th Aug., 1918	11th Sept., 1918
Warcup, G.	120602	—	9th Aug., 1918	12th Sept., 1918
Hill, H.	76231	—	18th Aug., 1918	13th Jan., 1919
Cox, J.	115984	—	26th Aug., 1918	18th Jan., 1919
Moses, J.	142984	—	13th Sept., 1918	21st Nov., 1918
Webb, J. A.	92231	—	13th Sept., 1918	23rd Oct., 1918
Marshall, F. W.	119379	—	30th Sept., 1918	3rd Feb., 1919
Yarwood, H.	160258	—	30th Sept., 1918	3rd Feb., 1919
Herbert, A. G.	36510	—	3rd Oct., 1918	1st Feb., 1919
Allen, G.	181692	—	3rd Oct., 1918	1st Feb., 1919
Moore, E. B.	103877	—	3rd Oct., 1918	21st Oct., 1918
Gibbins, G.	29475	—	6th Oct., 1918	13th Jan., 1919
Collyen, H.	168354	—	18th Oct., 1918	3rd Feb., 1919
Thursfield, P. W.	164949	—	18th Oct., 1918	1st Feb., 1919
Fleming, F. S.	82246	—	29th Oct., 1918	1st Feb., 1919
Stodgill, A. H.	142373	—	4th Nov., 1918	16th Nov., 1918
Honeywill, S. J.	203331	—	7th Nov., 1918	3rd Feb., 1919
Warner, B. J.	96696	—	22nd Dec., 1918	3rd Feb., 1919
Madeley, W. F.	134663	—	22nd Dec., 1918	3rd Feb., 1919
Haley, E.	114738	—	24th Dec., 1918	3rd Feb., 1919
West, G.	285661	—	5th Jan., 1919	3rd Feb., 1919
Hucker, W. H.	299971	—	5th Jan., 1919	3rd Feb., 1919
Douglas, P.	L.6208	—	30th Jan., 1919	3rd Feb., 1919
Macnamara, N. N.	L.9186	—	30th Jan., 1919	3rd Feb., 1919
Eaton, T.	189038	—	30th Jan., 1919	3rd Feb., 1919
Cooper, G. E.	241847	—	30th Jan., 1919	3rd Feb., 1919

8.—PRIVATES (1ST CLASS).

Name.	Regimental No.	From	Joined.	Left.
Foster, J.	G.P.6308	—	22nd Jan., 1917	13th Dec., 1918
Hewitt, A.	33924	—	23rd Feb., 1917	21st Jan., 1919
Smith, W.	54233	—	11th Mar., 1917	14th Nov., 1918
Saville, W.	80264	—	22nd June, 1917	13th Jan., 1919
Moore, T. J.	92429	—	17th Sept., 1917	3rd Feb., 1919
Barber, A.	63483	—	31st Mar., 1918	5th Nov., 1918
Hooley, F.	86868	—	31st Mar., 1918	22nd Dec., 1918
Geary, W. E.	11436	—	7th April, 1918	28th Nov., 1918
Towers, R.	93042	—	12th May, 1918	Cadre.
Baker, R. E.	213967	—	28th Dec., 1918	3rd Feb., 1919

9.—PRIVATES (2ND CLASS).

Name.	Regimental No.	From	Joined.	Left.
Robinson, A. J. T.	79680	3 a.m.	15th June, 1917	Jan., 1919
Williamson, S.	P.44296	—	25th Feb., 1918	27th Oct., 1918
Wetten, E. J.	125962	—	5th April, 1918	Cadre.
Bussell, F. J.	163706	—	25th Nov., 1918	31st Jan., 1919
Hutchinson, J. B.	294886	—	24th Dec., 1918	1st Feb., 1919

† Killed since leaving No. 24 Squadron. ‡ Died since leaving No. 24 Squadron.

OFFICERS' ADDRESSES.

ABRAHAMS, G., c/o. Craftsman Film Laboratory, 251, West 19th Street, New York, U.S.A.
ALLANSON, E. L., Griggithston Hill, 8, Park Avenue, Scarborough.
ALLEN, R. C., Belfield, Windermere.
ANDREWS, Major J. O., D.S.O., M.C., c/o. Cox & Co., Bombay.
ARNOT, Captain T. C., 6, Dryburgh Gardens, Kelvinside, Glasgow.
ARONSON, J. G., Box 983, Durban, S.A.

BAIR, H. L., D.F.C., 907, Broadway, New York City, U.S.A.
BALMER, H. F., 917, Dovercourt Road, Toronto, Ont.
BARLOW, N. H., Christchurch, New Zealand.
BARTON, Captain H. D., D.F.C., Matabiele, East Griqualand, S.A.
BEAUCHAMP, F. E., Meyronne, Sask., Canada.
BELL, J. W., 8, Grafton Street, Charbattetown, Canada.
BISSONETTE, C. A., 1063, los Polas Street, los Angelos, California.
BLOFIELD, B. L., Woodlands, Sydenham Hill, London, S.E.
BLOOM, A. L., Kirkby Mount, Beechwood E., Harrogate, Yorks.
BREEN, P. P., 15, Waterloo Road, Dublin, Ireland.
BRIDGEWATER, R. D., 174, Holland Park Road, London, W.
BRINDLE, P., Brindon Cottage, Lostock, Bolton, Lancs.
BROWN, Captain A. J., M.C., St. Neots, London Road, Deal.
BURCHER, Captain L. C., Council Offices, Cleobury Mortimer, Salop.
BURT, P. H., 49, Lonsdale Road, Harborne, Birmingham.
BUTLER, C., Cranford, Burley in Wharfedale, Yorks.

CAPON, Captain R. S., 33, Southlands Road, Bromley Common, Bromley, Kent.
CARRUTHERS, Captain D., Kingston, Ont., Canada.
CLIFTON, E. N., 12, Cambridge Square, London, W.
COCKERELL, S., 141, Thornbury Road, Osterly Park, Middlesex.
COPELAND, H. T. H., c/o. Air Ministry.
COWPER, Captain A. K., M.C., c/o. Commercial Bank of Sydney, Exchange Branch, Pitt Street, Sydney, N.S.W.
CRESWELL, A. A., Kisbey, Sask., Canada.
CROSBEE, C. H., 79, Greenfield Road, Harborne, Birmingham.
CROSSEN, E. P., Sunderland, Ont., Canada.
CRUTCH, J. H., Wickham Way, Beckenham, London, S.E.

DALRYMPLE, Captain S., Australian Estates and Mortgage Co., 96, Leandenhall St., London, E.C.
DAVIES, Captain R. C,. Bodfor, Aberdovey, Wales.
DYNES, R. S. J., 658, Fairholme Road, Barons Court, London, W.

ELDRIDGE, R. A., 18, York Road, New Southgate, London, N.
EVANS, D. E., Great Hoxmead Bury, Buntingford.
EVANS, H. V., Naini Tal, Gap Road, Wimbledon, London, S.W. 19.
EVERISS, E. W., South Field, Woodchester, Stroud, Glos.

FARRANT, L. G, 13, Elm Road, Woodney, Rock Ferry, Cheshire.
FARRELL, Captain C. M. G., D.F.C., 1333, 15th Avenue, Regina, Sask., Canada.
FLANAGAN, J. V., 1803, Beacon Street, Brookline, Mass., U.S.A.
FORDHAM, R. G., Broom Hall, Biggleswade, Beds.
FORESTER, N. G., 401, Barnard Avenue, Vernon, B.C., Canada.
FOSTER, G. B., D.F.C., 8, Edgehill Avenue, Montreal, Canada.
FRANKISH, Captain J. R., Longham Hall, Longham, Yorks.
FULLER, R. U., 2, Warltersville Road, Hornsey Rise, London, N. 19.

GERAGHTY, W. G. C., 379, Elm Avenue, Westencourt, Montreal, P.Q., Canada.
GOODALL, J. H. H., The Vicarage, Rotherham, Yorks.

HALLAM, E. W., Mabelbank Broty, Ferry West, Dundee, N.B.
HAMMERSLEY, Captain R. G., Avenue House, Measham, near Ashby-de-la-Zouch.
HARRIES, T. M., D.F.C., Chagnaramas Estate, Point Gourdie, Trinidad, B.W.I.
HAZELL, Major T. F., D.S.O., M.C., D.F.C., R.A.F. Club.
HEAKES, F. V., 489, Euclid Avenue, Toronto, Canada.
HELLETT, T. T. B., Astcourt, Natal, S.A., and c/o. National Bank of S.A., Erens Place, London, E.C.
HENDRIE, E. T., Woodcroft, Birbeck Road, Sidcup, Kent.
HEPBURN, Captain A., 105, Weston Street, Brunswick, Victoria, Australia, and c/o. C. W. Swaffield ,134, Cheapside, London, E.C.
HISTED, J. E., Arney Road, RemKere, Auckland, New Zealand.
HOWARD, M. L., 15, Center Street, New Haven, Conn., U.S.A.
HUGHES-CHAMBERLAIN, Major R. E. A. W., 11, Bedford Row, London, W.C. 1.
HUNTER, G. F., 87, High Street, Clapham, London, S.W.

IVES, Captain W. B., Holmehurst, Rawdon, Leeds.

OFFICERS' ADDRESSES.—*Contd.*

JACKSON, J. W., 171, Shaftsbury Avenue, London, W.C.
JAFFRAY, Sir W. E., Bart., Skilts, Redditch.
JAMES, Captain W. F. T., Penydarren House, Merthyr Tydvil, Wales.
JEPHSON, J. H., Myton, Ene Avenue, Lewes, Sussex.
JOHNSON, Captain G. O., M.C., 15, Norwich Avenue, Woodstock, Ont., Canada, and 41, Seaford Road, Eastbourne.
JOHNSON, P. W., 44, Windsor Road, Finchley, London, N. 3.
JOHNSTON, E. G., Mount Street, Perth, West Australia.
JONES, Major H. W. G., Garth, Portardawn, South Wales.

KEARY, C. R., Northwood Cottage, Clayton, Newcastle, Staffs.
KENT, R. F. J., 3rd D. Guards, Sialk of Punjab, India.
KER, R. H. B., Kershaugh, Victoria, B.C., Canada.

LAMBERT, W. C., D.F.C., 318, Hepler Street, Ironton, Ohio, U.S.A.
LARRABEE, E. P., Bellingham, State of Washington.
LAWRENCE, J. A., Cookstown, Ont., Canada.
LAWSON, Captain E. A. C., M.C., 2, Virginia Road, Leeds, Yorks.
LERWILL, O., Newbury House, Combemartin, Devon.
LINDEBURG, E. W., 13, Elmbank Street, Glasgow.
LINDO, G. M., 120A, Westbourne Terrace, London, W.
LONG, Major S. H., D.S.O., M.C., Bebington, Cheshire.
LONGTON, Captain W. H., D.F.C., A.F.C., c/o. Air Ministry.
LOWE, Captain C. N., M.C., D.F.C., c/o. Barclay's Bank, Maida Vale, N.W.

MACDOUGALL, P. A., M.C., Scalloway, Shetland Isles.
MARK, Captain R. T., M.C., Ettrick, Grove Road, Gosforth, Northumberland.
MCCRACKEN, H. J., Austenville, Bloomfield, Belfast, Ireland.
MCDONALD, Captain I. D. R., M.C., D.F.C., 57, Havard Road, Gunnersbury, London, W. 4.
MCKAY, A. E., Cobalt, Ontario, Canada.
MCMURTRIE, E. G., The Braes, Arthur Street, Ashfield, Syndey, N.S.W.
MENZIES, J. T., 43, Nethergate, Dundee, N.B.
MIDDLEBROOK, N., Beechwood Grove, Ilkley, Yorks.
MOORE, Major A. G., M.C., 47, Knightsbridge, Hyde Park Corner, London, S.W. 1.
MORGAN, W. A. C., M.C., 28, York Gardens, Clifton, Bristol.

NIXON, W. E., Winsten Vic., Matlock, Derby.

PALMER, Captain J., 131, Verdoorn Street, Pretoria, S.A.
PASSMORE, F. S., 83, Brunswick Avenue, Toronto, Canada.
POPE, Captain S. L. G., Connemara, Valencia Road, Worthing, Sussex.
POWELL, O. G., 14, Kent Road, Southsea, Hants.

RABAGLIATI, Lieut.-Colonel C. E. C., M.C., Tatmore Place, Hitchin, Herts.
RALSTON, Captain J. S., M.C., 31, Snowden Place, Stirling, Scotland.
RICHARDSON, H. B., M.C., 114, Woodstock Road, Oxford.
ROBERTSON, Captain B. K. D., A.F.C., 26, Linden Road, Redlands, Bristol.
ROBERTSON, G. P. Whitmore Lodge, Wolverhampton.
ROBESON, Major V. A. H., M.C., The Abbey Cottage, Tewkesbury, Glos.
ROCHE, C., 4, Uxbridge Road, Hanwell, London, W. 7.
ROCHE-KELLY, W., 20, St. Stephen's Green, Dublin, Ireland.
RORISON, J. C., 627, West 115th Street, New York City, U.S.A.
ROSE, R. K., Kilravock, Harewood Road, S. Croydon, Surrey.

SAUNDBY, Captain R. H. M. S., M.C., The Tower House, Harrow-on-the-Hill.
SEDGWICK, F. B., 119, Piccadilly, London, W.
SELWYN, Captain W., D.F.C., Toadsmoor House, Stroud, Glos.
SEYMOUR, H. J. C., Castle Buildings, Rugby.
SHARP, R. B., Auburn Street, Manchester.
SHARPE, Captain T. S., Cunthorpe, Tuffley, Glos.
SHUTER, G. W., 91, Shooter's Hill Road, Blackheath, London, S.E.
SIMMERS, V. H., 1261½, Yonge Street, Toronto, Canada.
SLIPPER, R. A., Avondale Park, Walmer Road, Kensington, London, W.
SOUTHEY, J. H., Hillmoor, Steynsburg, Cape Province, S.A.
STATHAM, W. H., Morstrand, Ashby-de-la-Zouch, Leicester.
STEFANSSON, B., Suite 11, Nava Villa, Winnipeg, Canada.
SUTHERLAND, D., 21, Rose Avenue, Toronto ,Canada.
SUTTON, A. W., Scotland Road, Stanwix, Carlisle.
SWART, Major J. G., M.C., 55, Trentham Road, Longton, Staffs.

TAYLOR, A., Spenser, Idaho, U.S.A.
THOMSON, W. B., Thamesville, Toronto, Canada.
TIDMARSH, Captain D. M., M.C., Lota, Limerick, Ireland.
TUBBS, H. V. L., Claremont, Whetstone, London, N.

UNDERHILL, R. J., Moline, Manitoba, Canada.

WALES, G. E., 50, Austen Avenue, Nottingham.
WARNER, W. F., 103, Winchester Street, Merivale, Christchurch, N.Z.
WATKINS, J. R. Holmesdale, Eaton Crescent, Swansea.
WATSON, F. L., 225, 4th Avenue, Ottawa, Canada.
WATTS, Captain F. M. I., Laureston Lodge, Newton Abbot, Devon.
WHITEHEAD, G. H., 21, Truro Road, Wavertree, Liverpool.
WIGAN, A. P. C. W., Penair, Church Road, Whitchurch, Cardiff, S. Wales.
WILKINSON, Lieut.-Colonel A. M., D.S.O., 14, Creffield Road, Ealing, London, W.
WILSON, E. B., 7, Ashworth Mansions, Elgin Avenue, Maida Vale, London, W. 9.
WOOD, H. A., 54, Oakmount Road, Toronto, Canada.
WOODHAMS, C. E., 18, Malham Grove, East Dulwich, London, S.E.
WOODS, J. R., 109, Barcombe Avenue, Streatham Hill, London, S.W.
WOOLLETT, Captain H. W., D.S.O., M.C., Cardigan Lodge, Newmarket, Cambs.
WREN, A., Birkenshaw, Langbank, Renfrewshire.
WRIGHT, E. F., The College, Potchefstroom, Transvaal, S.A.

YOUNG, H. A., 1, Arundel Villas, Page Road, Clacton-on-Sea, Essex.
YOUNGMAN, H. J., Easterdon, Victoria, Australia.

ADDRESSES—OTHER RANKS.

ADDISON, S. F., 37, Canning Street, Kempstown, Brighton, Sussex.
ALLAN, W. A. S., 21, Miller Crescent, Edinburgh.
AMOS, A., 1, Belgrave Terrace, Corstorphine, Midlothian.
ASHBY, R. E., "Bedmond," Kings Langley, Herts.
ATKIN, W., 34, Leighton Street, St. Carlton Road, Notts.
AYLING, F. H., The Cottage, Warnham, Sussex.

BARBER, A., 115, Dale House Fold, Poynton, near Stockport.
BENTLEY, F., 6, Anne of Cleves Road, Dartford, Kent.
BISHOP, C., 29, Grove Road, Seven Oaks, Kent.
BLANCHARD, F., 62, London Road, East Grinstead, Sussex.
BLOWER, G. W., 152, Wendover Road, Staines, Middx.
BOND, C., 236, Oak Street, Abingdon, Berks.
BRADBURY, L., 10, Lancaster Street, Mossley, Manchester.
BRAND, O. W. S., 3, Albion Square, Dalston, Surrey.
BROOKS, W. D., 145, Ashford Road, Eastbourne, Sussex.
BROWN, H., High Street, Wyke Regis, Weymouth, Dorset.
BROWN, L. C., Arnold Hill, Leeds, Maidstone.
BROWN, S. F. C., 12, Lawrenny Street, Neyland, Pembrokeshire.
BROWNING, L., 17, Morley Terrace, Leekhampton, Cheltenham, Glos.
BULSTRODE, S., School Hill, Bishops Waltham, Hants.
BURFORD, E., 16, Great Bridge Street, West Bromwich, Staffs.
BURRELL, S. A., 50, Anesty Road, West Ham, London, E.

CALLOWAY, J., 2, Ocherill Street, Tipton, Staffs.
CARRUTHERS, J. R., Scout View, Mossley, Manchester.
CHORLEY, E., 85, Hingiston Street, Birmingham.
CLARK, C. O. B., 6, Coleraine Road, Blackheath, London, S.E.
COCKERELL, S., 141, Thornbury Road, Osterly Park, Middx.
COCKERTON, E. C., 248, Grove Green Road, Leytonstone, Essex.
COCKRELL, W. F., Alma Cottage, Shalford, near Guildford, Surrey.
COCKS, A. F., Post Office Street, Tuskington, Lincs.
COOK, E., 42, Armayer Road, Shepherd's Bush, London, W.
COOPER, B. C., 15, Newcastle Street, Silverdale, Staffs.
COOPER, H., 3, St. Faith's Villas, Hitchin, Herts.
COTTERELL, C. C., 193, London Road, Reading.
COX, E. G., 46, Wellon Road, Ilford, Essex.
COX, F. S., 24, Stibb Green, Burbage, Marlborough, Wilts.
COX, J. L., 9, Hastings Road, Maidstone, Kent.
COX, L. C., The Laurels, Boldmere Road, Erdington, Birmingham.
COXALL, A. C., 32, Lowman Road, Holloway, London, N.W.
CRAGHILL, J. H., 2, Brooklands Terrace, Sayers Street, Huntingdon.
CREWDSON, A., 9, Eden Street, Blackpool, Lancs.
CRITCHLEY, E., 84, Standishgate, Wigan, Lancs.
CROFTS, S., 104, Norfolk Road, Margate, Kent.
CRONAN, P., 6, Lower Bridge Street, Dublin, Ireland.
CUNLIFFE, H. L., 22, Wargraive Road, Earlstown, Lancs.

DA COSTA, S., 20, Gainsborough Road, Bow, London, E.

DAINTY, W. J., 16, Wharfedale St., Wednesday.
DALLEY, R. H., 91, Norroy Road, Putney, London, S.W.
DAVIES, G., 5, Laistridge Court, Bradford, Yorks.
DAWS, G., 45, Avondale Road, Mortlake, London, S.W.
DAY, E. C., Penn, High Wycombe, Bucks.
DEARDEN, J. H., Trelawny, King Alfred Place, Winchester, Hants.
DEARMAN, E., 8, Eldon Street, Sheffield.
DENNIS, J. W., 5, Fontonoy Road, Balham, London, S.W.
DETHRIDGE, A. J., 15, Copley Street, Aston, Birmingham.
DODGSON, F. S., 30, Park View, Crosby, Liverpool.
DOW, A., 60, Dunard Street, Glasgow.
DUNBAR, W., 13, George Street, Whitchurch, Glasgow.
DUNS, R. A., 231, Sherrard Road, Manor Park, Essex.
DUTNALL, H., 23, Burley Road, Sittingbourne, Kent.
DYER, W. H., 158, Dames Road, Forest Gate, London, E. 7.

EARNEY, H. A., 30, Nursery Road, Salisbury, Wilts.
EATOCK, H., 89, Church Street, Bolton, Lancs.
EDWARDS, H., 5, Barker Street, Nantwich, Cheshire.
ELGY, B. C. H., Crewdson Road, Brixton Road, London, S.W.
ELLIOTT, S. W., 109, Carlingford Road, West Green, London, N.
ELLIS, F. P., 26, Acme Road, Watford, Herts.
ELLIS, J. C., 77, Lower Rushton Road, Hornbury, Bradford, Yorks.
ELSOM, L., 9, Raywood Villas, Wellsted Street, Hull, Yorks.
EVANS, W. L., Cartriff, Llangbyther, Carmarthen, Wales.
EVENS, E., 182, Pearl Street, Roath, Cardiff.
EVERSFIELD, J., Holly Cottage, Wateringbury, Maidstone, Kent.
EXTON, H. J., 84, Kent Road, Swindon, Wilts.

FISHER, A. J., M.S.M., 58, Roupell Street, Blackfriars, London, S.E.
FISHER, F., 24, East Street, Wolverhampton, Staffs.
FITZMAURICE, M., 59, Ingestre Buildings, Ingestre Place, London, W.
FLATLEY, W., 13, Duncan Street, Liverpool.
FLEET, B. S., 215, Ludlow Road, Itchen, Southampton, Hants.
FLEMING, G. H., Elm Mead, Victoria Road, Newport, I. of W.
FLOOK, F., Station Road, Winterbourne Down, near Bristol.
FOSTER, J., 17, St. Paul's Road, Nelson, Lancs.
FRENCH, W. L., "Leigham," York Road, Woking, Surrey.
FROST, G. Y., Winchelsea, Reigate, Surrey.

GARDINER, J. R., M.S.M., c/o. Air Ministry.
GARLAND, L., 85A, Melbourne Grove, East Dulwich, London, S.E.
GASCOYNE, P., 153, Westfield Lane, Mansfield, Notts.
GAZARD, F. H., 3, Speilmans Road, Radborough, Stroud, Glos.
GEARY, W. E., 32, Astley Road, Hemel Hempstead, Herts.
GEORGE, W. A., 80, Grove Road, Kings Heath, Birmingham.
GIBSON, E. J., 146, Gordon Road, Strood, Kent.
GIBSON, W., 23, Brunswick Street, Belfast, Ireland.
GILLIES, P., Glensburg, Brightons, Polmont, Scotland.
GLADSTONE, P., 31, Walpole Road, Wimbledon, London, S.W. 19.
GLEDHILL, S., 4, Prince Street, Gilbert Street, Halifax, Yorks.
GOLDSTEIN, J., 93, Burdett Avenue, Westcliffe-on-Sea, Essex.
GOODWILL, F., 25, Fairfield Road, Bridlington, Yorks.
GOY, W. S., 14, Independant Street, Radford, Notts.
GRADWELL, V., 10, Knowles Street, Radcliffe, Lancs.
GREEN, A. G., 132, Risley Avenue, Wood Green, London, N.
GREEN, W., 44, Burrard Road, Hampstead, London, N.W.

GREENAWAY, W., 6, North Avenue, Exeter, Devon.
GREENHALGH, F., 26, Rhode Street, Tottington, Bury, Lancs.
GRIEVE, W., Church Street, Stenhousemuir, Larbert, Scotland.
GRINTON, T., Fire Station, Laureston Place, Edinburgh.
GROOME, J., 2, Vine Square Mews, Eastbourne, Kent.

HAINES, G., Perrystone Hill, Yatton, near Ross, Herefordshire.
HALLAM, F., 143, Radcliffe Street, Oldham, Lancs.
HAMMOND, J. G., 20, Dale Street, Blackpool, Lancs.
HAMPSON, J., Cambridge Road, Southport, Lancs.
HARDESTY, S., 27, Grafton Street, Worksop, Notts.
HARLAND, S. F., 91, Cardiff Road, Reading, Berks.
HARPER, A., 22, Corporation Buildings, Farringdon Road, London, E.C.
HARTLEY, B., 48, Southampton Road, Kentish Town, London, N.

HARTNELL, A. G., 33, Westgate Street, Taunton, Somerset.
HAWES, H., 60, Royal Park Road, Leeds, Yorks.
HAWKESFORD, S., 181, Ash Road, Saltley, Birmingham.
HENDERSON, C., 55, Byford Street, Liverpool.
HEWITT, A., 5, Vetch Street, York Road, Leeds, Yorks.
HICKEY, A., 97, Felsham Road, Putney, London, W.
HILL, H., 3, Ardock Road, Catford, London, S.E. 6.
HINTON, F. M., 28, Albert Road, Handsworth, Birmingham.
HIPWELL, J. T., Kettering Road, Geddington, Northants.
HOBSON, H. E., Sea Farm, Gramthorpe, Lincs.
HOOLEY, F., 8, Wheat Street, Ashton-under-Lyne.
HOSKINS, V. E. T., 16, Rookery Terrace, Mantle Street, Wellington, Somerset.
HOWARD, C. W. J., 30, Meyrick Road, Battersea, London, S.W.
HOWARD, H., 93, Park Road, Plumstead, London, S.E.
HOWE, A., 249, Blackfriars Road, Dundee.
HULME, A., Ryles Mount, Ryles Park, Macclesfield, Cheshire.
HUMMERSTONE, G., 26, York Street, Walworth, London, S.E.
HUMPHRIES, E. J., 136, Furborough Road, Earls Court, London, S.W.
HUMPHRIES, E. L., North Road, Gandhurst, Kent.
HURRELL, F. S., The Box, Danbury, near Chelmsford, Essex.
HURST, C. G., 13, Prospect Place, Woolwich, London, S.E.
HUTCHINSON, J. B., 41, Hampton Road, Teddington, Kent.

IBBETSON, W. T., 7, Hook Road, Goole, Yorks.
INGRAM, H., Wilton, near Burton-on-Trent, Staffs.
ISTED, C. H., 23, Upper High Street, Worthing, Sussex.

JAMIE, E., 4, Ramsey Street, Montrose, Scotland.
JEFFERSON, B., 27, Wye Terrace, Tottenham, Bishop Auckland, Durham.
JENKINS, H. L., Prince Albert Hotel, Garnant, Carmarthen.
JENKINSON, P., 55, Victoria Road, Fenton, Stoke-on-Trent.
JEWELL, W. C., 27, Shandon Road, Clapham Park, London, S.W.
JOHNSON, W. J., 97, Watson Street, Birkenhead, Cheshire.
JONES, G. W., 40, Shakespeare Street, Sparkhill, Birmingham.
JONES, W., Low Bar, Newport, Shropshire.

KING, D. W., near Running Mase, Galleywood Common, Chelmsford, Essex.
KING, E. J. A, 74, Whitehouse Crescent, Bedminster, Bristol.
KING, L. C., 34, New Park Street, Devizes, Wilts.
KIRBY, C. A., 5, Franklin Road, Watford, Herts.

LACEY, J., 120, Moulsham Street, Chelmsford, Essex.
LAMPARD, T. S., Prospect Villas, Oxenden, near Farnham, Surrey.
LANGSTON, J. H., 11, Henry Place, St. John's Wood, London, N.W.
LEE, F. R. V., 46, Clarendon Street, Oxford.
LEES, E., c/o. Mr. W. Hurry, Whaley Lane, Whaley Bridge, Ches.
LENG, W. F., 8, Knesborough Road, Ripon, Yorks.
LEVY, J. 107, Mildmay Grove, Mildmay Park, London, N.
LEWIS, F. T., 5, Corringway Street, Golders Green, London ,N.W.
LINTER, H. G., 43, Cockshoot Road, Reigate, Surrey.
LOCKE, H., 38, St. George's Street, Macclesfield, Cheshire.
LOVELL, G. H., 6, Holkham House, Sulgrave Road, Hammersmith, London, W.
LUSCOMBE, J., 12, Tavistock Road, Harlesden, London, N.W.
LUSTY, W. D., Ivy Cottage, Selsby, Stroud, Glos.

MACKLIN, T., 86, St. Mark's Road, Salisbury, Wilts.
MARHSALL, E., 150, Portnall Road, Harrow Road, London, N.W.
MARTIN, W., 4, Broadfield Cottages, Wadeshill, Winchmore Hill, N.
MATTHEWS, G. H., "Fairlea," 1st Avenue, Bush Hill Park, London, N.W.
MAYBOURNE, T., Windmill Inn, Preston, near Faversham, Kent.
McKENZIE, R., 2, Albert Place, Inverness, Scotland.
MEALL, F., 133, Lowson Street, Liverpool.
MEEK, H. M., "Lynwood," Willoughby Road, Langley, Bucks.
MILLER, J., 21, Glasford Street, Flemington, Motherwell, Lanark.
MILLS, G., 113, Pemberton Street, Cheetham, Manchester.
MOORE, T. J., Cove, near Farnborough, Hants.
MOORES, W. R., 7, St. John's Road, Uxbridge, Middx.
MOREY, B., 16, Twyford Avenue, Stainshaw, Portsmouth, Hants.
MORGAN, T. J., Tregoes Cottage, Fishguard, Pembrokeshire.
MORLEY, C., 149, Lansfield Street, Queen's Park, London, N.W.
MORRIS, A., 2, Oxford Gardens, Chiswick, London, W.
MORRIS, J. W., 10, Gresse Street, Tottenham, London, N.

MORRISON, J. E., 5, Penwell Road, Holloway, London, N.
MUNDAY, A. J., 79, Stafford Street, Swindon Wilts.
MYHILL, S. C., 23, Albany Street, Regents Park, London, W.
MYRAM, J., 19, Mill Lane, Dorking, Surrey.

NEAL, E., Long Wittenham, Abingdon, Berks.
NEWSTEAD, F., 21 Wenthorpe Road, Putney, London, S.W.
NICHOLLS, H. E., 4, Dean Cottages, Tartan Hill, Cobham, Surrey.
NIXON, G. W., 2, Shelton New Road, Stoke-on-Trent.
NOBLE, S. R., 149, Alexander Road, Grimsby, Lincs.

OADES, A. C., 26, Summerstown, Lower Tooting, London, S.W.
OGDEN, J., 15, Fountain Street, Park Lane, Leeds, Yorks.
OLIVER, A. R., Kingswood Common, Henley-on-Thames, Oxford.
ORR, J., Duntreath, Blackness Road, Dundee, Scotland.

PARK, W. H., Police Station, Milenthorpe, Westmoreland.
PARRY, H. L., Smithy House, Marford, near Wrexham, Denbigh.
PARSONS, G. A., 101, Arthur Street, Small Heath, Birmingham.
PATRICK, H., 28, Coach Row, Bradford Moor, Bradford, Yorks.
PAULING, A., Culverton Farm, near Princes Risborough, Berks.
PAYNE, E., Hawarden House, Peddletrentide, Dorset.
PAYNE, R., Wymondham, Oakham, Rutland.
PEAT, D. D., 10, Lockrin Place, Edinburgh.
PERCY, R. A. E., 17, Law Street, Rochdale, Lancs.
PERRY, J., 2, Ivy Terrace, Addington, Liskeard, Cornwall.
PETERS, G. H., 12, Gladstone Avenue, Wood Green, London, N.
PIPE, A. H. A., 27, Castle Street, Shetford, Norfolk.
POLLOCK, D. N., 142, Holland Street, Glasgow.
PONSFORD, F. W., 23, Marlborough Road, Portsea, Portsmouth, Hants.
POPPLETON, S., 128, Milton Street, Walsall, Staffs.
PORTER, G., 27, Blakeston Street, Fleetwood, Lancs.
POTTS, J. H., 31, Bridge Street, Wednesbury, Staffs.
PRINGLE, H., 66, Buchanan Street, Stockton-on-Tees, Durham.
PRINGLE, H. G., Palmerston North, N.Z.
PRITCHARD, W. P., 34, Ward Avenue, Fulham Palace Road, London, S.W. 6.
PUGH, A. F., 11, Caroline Street, Camden Town, London, N.W.
PULLAR, S. W., 27, Alcester Street, Stoke, Devonport, Devon.

QUINSEY, W. J. 45, Dulby Road, Wandsworth, London, S.W.

RANDALL, T., 13, North Street, Bradford Road, Dewsbury, Yorks.
REEVES, A., 155, Cambridge Road, Smethwick, Staffs.
REID, G. M., 6, Byfield Street, Radford, Notts.
RICHARDSON, L., 19, South Street, Gateshead-on-Tyne.
RILEY, P., 179, North Road, Clayton, Manchester.
RIMMER, G. B., 36, Bable Street, Formby, Liverpool.
ROBINSON, A. J. T., 14, Scyllor Road, Peckham Rye, London, S.E.
ROBINSON, A. R., Mistletoe Place, Reservoir Road, Egbaston, Birmingham.
ROSE, W. A., Saham Road, Walton, Norfolk.
ROWLES, G. A., Newland, Witney, Oxon.
ROXBURGH, J. S., 5, Murchiston Grove, Edinburgh.
RUSSELL, W. G., 47, Dover Street, The Avenue, Southampton, Hants.
RYAN, W. H., Holt Street, Holt, near Trowbridge, Wilts.

SARGENT, G. H., 27, Penny Street, Weymouth, Dorset.
SAVILLE, W., 77, Sherrads Road, Forest Gate, Essex.
SCHOFIELD, F., M.S.M., 8, Hawke Street, Stalybridge, Cheshire.
SCOTT, A., 88, Walker Street, Hassle Road, Hull.
SCOTT, A., 30, King's Street, Newton Stewart, Wigtownshire.
SEARLE, R. V., 20, Park End Street, Oxford.
SHARP, I., 19, Rawallan Road, Munster Road. Fulham, London, S.W.
SHAW, C., 32, Rogers Road, Birmingham.
SHAW, T. A., 16, May Street, Salford, Manchester.
SIM, A., 9, Temple Park Crescent, Edinburgh.
SIMMONS, C. G., 14A, North Road, Richmond, Surrey.
SIMPSON, T., Donaghadie, Belfast, Ireland.
SKINNER, F., Durgates, Wadhurst, Sussex.
SLATER, J., 15, Eldon Place, Burgley, near Leeds, Yorks.
SLATER, J., 16, Barkston Place, Holbeck, Leeds, Yorks.
SLEET, W. J., Firs Road, Harehill, Ottershaw, Chertsey, Surrey.
SMITH, D. W., 36, Temple Road, Windsor, Berks.
SMITH, E. W., 29, Gainsborough Road, Finchley, London, N.

SMITH, J. W., The Cedars, New Moston, Failsworth, Manchester.
SMITH, N. J., 47, Upham Park Road, Chiswick, London, W.
SMITH, W., Upplegarth, Woodford, near Leeds, Yorks.
SMITH, W. E., 20, Ambergate Street, Kennington, London, S.E. 17.
SOOTHILL, F., Woodville, Leeds Road, Dewsbury, Yorks.
SPELLER, W. J., 30, Patshull Road, Kentish Town, London, N.
SPENCER, T., 3, Jones Square, Hempshaw Lane, Stockport, Cheshire.
STEAD, C., 103, Hall Lane, Bradford, Yorks.
STEPHEN, G. A., 3, Devanah Terrace, Aberdeen, Scotland.
STEVENSON, S. W., 73, Longfellow Road, Bow, London, E.
STIRLING, J. W., 28, Mayfield Terrace, Edinburgh.
STOW, S. L., 93, Ponting Street, Swindon, Wilts.

TAIT, H. J., The Green, Cottingham, near Hull, Yorks.
TANNER, R., 26, Viola Street, Bootle, Liverpool.
TEALBY, F. R. V., 25, Shakespeare Street, Loughborough, Notts.
THOMAS, A., 17, Trenyrick Street, Pembroke Dock, Cardiff.
THOMAS, C., 32, Gloucester Street, Cardiff.
THOMAS, S. C., 31, Thomas Street, Averavon, Glamorgan.
THOMPSON, J., The Hawthorns, East Halton, Lincs.
THORNBURGH, W., 38, Wharf Road, Notting Hill, London, N.W.
THOULD, F. J., Old Street, Upton-on-Severn, Worcs.
TILLEY, E., 2, Leigh Road, Wimborne, Dorset.
TINGLE, A. W., "Elmhurst," Stanley Road, Leicester.
TOPLEY, C. L., 2, Camrose Street, Plumstead, London, S.E. 18.
TOWERS, R., 1, Dundonald Street, Preston, Lancs.
TREAVIS, W. A., 10, Marion Terrace, Dorchester.

UNDERWOOD, J., 73, George Street, Farncombe, Surrey.

VALENTINE, J. H., 78, Bancroft Road, Hitchin, Herts.
VINCENT, W. B., 2, Bishopstone Road, Gloucester.
VINYCOMBE, J. K., 74, Park Lane, Wallington, Surrey.

WAINER, G. W., 78, Childers Street, Hyde Park, Doncaster.
WALTON, F., Firwood, Lyme Grove, Thornton-le-Fylde, Lancs.
WALTON, H., 56, Albion Street, Nelson, Lancs.
WARD, C. F., 142, Park Avenue, Barking, Essex.
WARD, H., 31, Forge Lane, Bradford, Yorks.
WARD, S. E., 23, St. John's Place, Mansfield, Notts.
WEBB, A. V., Tidys Green, Limpsfield, Surrey.
WEBB, L., Trehawn, Rochester, Kent.
WEBSTER, S., 5, Croft Street, Salford, Manchester.
WEIR, A. H., Wood End, Corfu Road, Motherwell, Lanark.
WELCH, J. W., Ingleton, Greenhill, Weymouth, Dorset.
WELSH, W. C., 18, Shirley Road, Bedford Park, London, W.
WETTEN, E. G., 55, Crown Street, Reading, Berks.
WHEELER, L. E., 65, West Street, Havant, Hants.
WHITWORTH, J., 2, Kendall Road, Bolton, Lancs.
WILKINSON, A. J., Rock House, Upper Bourne, Farnham.
WILLIAMS, V., "Elmhurst," Westcombe Park Road, Blackheath, London, S.E.
WILLIAMSON, S., 106, Ashbridge Street, Liverpool.
WILSON, A., 22, Balmoral Terrace, Leeds, Yorks.
WILSON, A., Rosevale, Bishopton, by Glasgow.
WILSON, H., Tower Cottage, Herne, Kent.
WINCH, D. F., 93, Cowley Road, Ilford, Essex.
WINN, D., 61, Tivoli Place, Little Horton, Bradford, Yorks.
WINTER, A., The Moor, Lightwater, Bagshot, Surrey.
WOOD, B. L., 53, High Street, Uxbridge, Middx.
WOOD, S. J., Croft, Wainfleet, Lincs.
WOOLFENDEN, E. T., 5, High Bank, Denton, Manchester.
WOOLLEY, F., 18, Malton Street, Oldham, Lancs.
WORKMAN, C. H., 3, Mona Villas, Portfielf, Hereford.
WORMALD, F. E., 22, Dugdale Road, Coventry, Warwickshire.
WORN, F. L., 71, London Road, Ipswich, Suffolk.
WORTH, R., 84, Trinity Street, Oldham, Lancs.
WRIGHT, L., 48, Cross Bank Street, Oldham, Lancs.
WRIGHT, S. R., "Lyndhurst," Bingley, Yorks.

YARWOOD, A., 2, Parcel Street, Beswick, Manchester.
YOUNG, H. W., 225, Whitehorse Lane, South Norwood, London, S.E.

www.ingramcontent.com/pod-product-compliance
Ingram Content Group UK Ltd.
Pitfield, Milton Keynes, MK11 3LW, UK
UKHW052106270726
14058UKWH00005BA/658

9 781843 427773